Youth Soccer For Parents

A Wiley Brand

Youth Soccer For Parents

by Tom Dunmore

Youth Soccer For Parents For Dummies®

Published by: **John Wiley & Sons, Inc.**, 111 River Street, Hoboken, NJ 07030-5774, www.wiley.com

For general information on our other products and services, please contact our Customer Care Department within the U.S. at 877-762-2974, outside the U.S. at 317-572-3993, or fax 317-572-4002. For technical support, please visit https://hub.wiley.com/community/support/dummies.

Wiley publishes in a variety of print and electronic formats and by print-on-demand. Some material included with standard print versions of this book may not be included in e-books or in print-on-demand. If this book refers to media that is not included in the version you purchased, you may download this material at http://booksupport.wiley.com. For more information about Wiley products, visit www.wiley.com.

Library of Congress Control Number: 2025930430

ISBN 978-1-394-29383-4 (pbk); ISBN 978-1-394-29385-8 (ebk); ISBN 978-1-394-29384-1 (ebk)

SKY10099379_030625

Contents at a Glance

Table of Contents

Introduction

From toddlers to teenagers, the world of youth soccer encompasses millions of players, and if you've picked up this book, your own child may well be joining or already involved in the sport. Those millions of kids play in thousands of different programs, leagues, and tournaments with all kinds of different names, purposes, and costs to you as a parent.

Youth Soccer For Parents For Dummies is your guide for any child's journey through soccer, from the first tentative kicks of a 2-year-old to looking at college soccer programs and scholarships.

While each of these millions of kids are one of many on a team, every young player is different and needs guidance on finding the right level of play, whether pursuing the game just for fun and friendship or aiming for competitive games. That's where this book can help in every aspect of parenting a youth soccer player.

About This Book

Every time you're faced with a big decision about what to do when it comes to your child's soccer, I hope you will pick up this book. You don't necessarily need to read it from cover to cover; instead, each chapter provides information on a key area of a young player's journey in the game.

Whether it's the choice between playing recreational or competitive soccer, looking for tips on how to practice and get better outside of organized team play, or understanding how to move between clubs, just turn to the chapter relevant to what could be more than a decade of your child playing the game.

In fact, I hope the information in this book can help guide choices and perspective on youth soccer to keep your kid playing longer and enjoying the "beautiful game" at its best. Youth soccer's structures and costs can be confusing and daunting, which is why this book exists: to help you better understand the pathways to maximize fun and develop soccer skills, friendships, and good health habits that soccer can provide every young player.

Foolish Assumptions

Perhaps you've never kicked a soccer ball — or maybe you were a good player yourself. Either way, this book will walk you through what can be a challenging landscape of youth soccer with so many programs to consider.

You'll soon find that most other parents are also feeling their way through how best to manage their child's youth soccer experience. Some common questions and concerns include the following:

>> Where do I get started finding a good soccer program?

>> What's the difference between recreational and competitive soccer?

>> How should I behave on the sideline during a game?

>> What should I do outside of organized practice to help my kid get better at the game?

>> What's the right way to communicate with a coach and my child's club?

This book guides you through answers to these questions and hundreds of others you may have. I start with the assumption that you don't know anything about the world of youth soccer, whether you've played the game or not, but pretty soon you'll be up to speed on how to navigate your child's journey in the wonderful world of soccer.

Icons Used in This Book

To help you navigate through this book, keep an eye out for the following icons. You'll see them in the margins throughout the book. This is what it means when you see one of these little images:

TIP

This highlights small pieces of advice that can help you understand key information about the youth soccer world to help guide your parenting decisions.

REMEMBER

This information is particularly useful to remember. These nuggets will come in handy as a soccer parent, so pay close attention to them!

WARNING

This very rarely pops up, but pay notice when you see it as it'll prepare you for a specific situation to be aware of.

TECHNICAL STUFF

Fortunately, there aren't too many obscure terms in youth soccer, but occasionally you'll see a particular fact or term explained.

Beyond the Book

This book has more than enough information and guidance in it to get you well on the way to being a knowledgeable soccer parent, but you can find even more to delve into online at Dummies.com.

Check out this book's online Cheat Sheet, which includes helpful tips for parents such as do's and don'ts for game day, questions to ask before signing up for a program, and more. Head to www.dummies.com and type **Youth Soccer For Parents For Dummies Cheat Sheet** in the search box.

Where to Go from Here

It's time to kick off. If you're brand new to the game of soccer, you can start out by getting up to speed on the rules. Perhaps you already know the basics: If so, you can lean right into learning about programs to get your kid into the game.

If your child is older and looking at more advanced programs or wanting specialized training, feel free to skip ahead to those sections. Either way, there's plenty to dip into that'll up your game off the field while your child gets their game going on the field!

1

Taking the First Kicks

Chapter **1**

Getting into the World's Most Popular Sport

Soccer, the world's game. It's called that for a reason: No sport attracts more participants and followers across the globe. The soccer World Cup is watched by billions of people every four years, and superstars like Lionel Messi or Cristiano Ronaldo rival any celebrity in the world for their number of fans. (Ronaldo is the most followed human being in the world on Instagram, with 640 million followers!)

Why is soccer so popular? Well, for a start, it is very easy to play. It's also been called the simplest game because if you have a ball — or really, any spherical object — you basically have all the equipment you need to get out there and play. Throw down a couple of objects to craft a makeshift goal to score in, find a few friends, and you (and your child) can be playing on a field, street, or beach anywhere in the world right away.

This utter simplicity is what will make it easy for your kid to pick up the game of soccer as well. While America woke up later to the "world's game" than most countries, every town or city in America these days has a soccer team or league that your child can take part in (and in many cities, a bewildering number of options this book will help you parse through). You can also get your kids started yourself in the back yard or at a local park by just kicking around a ball for fun.

Adding Up the Benefits of Youth Soccer

So, why should your kid join the millions of soccer participants in the United States? Because it can provide a lifetime of fun and fitness, and a fantastic opportunity to follow and play a game so popular around the world.

Having fun and making friends

There is one cardinal rule to remember when your kid starts playing soccer: They are doing it primarily to have fun and burn off some of that excess energy almost every kid has. Don't worry about your kid being the next Cristiano Ronaldo. Very, very few of the millions of youth soccer participants will go on to become professional soccer players.

REMEMBER

The score doesn't *really* matter in youth soccer games. Some parents put far too much pressure on their kids to excel and win games — instead of allowing them to develop a pure love of the game. Far too often, this leads to teenagers who grew up enjoying the sport burning out under the pressure and spoiling that passion.

Soccer is ultimately all about the joy of the game. Making a good pass, saving a goal, scoring a "screamer" (a brilliant goal) — these are the moments that make kids light up with smiles. Because the ball is always moving in soccer, boredom rarely creeps in — and unlike with individual sports, that joy is shared immediately with others on their team.

In fact, soccer is a sport particularly dependent on teamwork to be successful, so it's a great way for children to learn the value of working together toward a common goal (pun intended!).

Perhaps even more importantly, playing on a team provides an instant opportunity to make a whole bunch of new friends. Your kid will be playing with a dozen plus other children at practices and at games, as well as likely soon spending time with them outside of soccer. Lifelong friendships are made on the soccer field.

Developing fitness and physical skills

Soccer is a great way for your kid to keep fit — and is definitely more fun than calisthenics. Running is integral to soccer in training and at games, developing stamina and burning off some of that childhood energy.

Coordination, endurance, and agility are three further key physical components of the game that your child can develop while playing the sport. The fun of soccer — chasing the ball in all sorts of directions — helps develop strong physical motor skills such as balance and acceleration without your kid even realizing it. Exercise that your kid finds fun and wants to do is certainly the best kind!

Over the long run, playing soccer frequently develops important physical skills including

>> **Coordination:** As with playing any ball game, soccer helps develop coordination between the eyes and body movements, responding to the moving object — the ball. Even though soccer players (except the goalkeeper) do not use their hands, the coordination required to "see ball, kick ball" helps develop skills that can transfer to other athletic activities or even playing an instrument.

>> **Balance:** Soccer is a sport particularly reliant on body control, because almost every movement in the sport requires getting into a balanced position. Players are constantly turning, changing direction, and reacting to

rapid movements of the ball — being able to pivot quickly and position the body to kick the ball effectively requires plenty of agility. Soccer players' balance has been compared to that of gymnasts.

>> **Speed and acceleration:** Soccer is one of the least stationary sports — compare it to baseball or (American) football — so your kid will be running a lot. And not just running a lot: Sprinting quickly after the ball and accelerating as fast as possible over short distances are critical parts of the sport. Playing soccer frequently will develop sprinting muscles and quickness.

>> **Strength:** Soccer isn't a sport in which lifting weights is necessarily a plus. But playing it will develop muscle and bone strength, lower body fat, and provide a great workout. This is particularly true for lower body muscles, such as hamstrings and quadriceps, and this can translate into improved athletic strength for other sports and everyday life.

>> **Stamina:** Few ball sports require as much running as soccer, with repeated short and long runs taking place in practices and games. Players are on their feet moving for prolonged periods of time. This helps develop endurance and is fantastic aerobic exercise!

Fortunately, while playing plenty of soccer helps develop all these physical attributes, this isn't a sport that only those supremely physically fit or those blessed with unusual size or strength can enjoy.

REMEMBER

A variety of body types and sizes can participate at recreational levels and excel at the elite level. Unlike for basketball, for example, height is not necessarily an advantage in soccer. Some of the best players in the sport's history, like Lionel Messi (5'7") and Diego Maradona (5'5"), are below the height of an average male. Guile, skill, and a low center of gravity can beat pure size and strength.

Different positions on the field suit different body sizes and shapes. Defenders playing in the center, where leaping and heading the ball may be called for, are often taller players, while a shorter but speedier player may be better suited for sprinting up and down the sideline.

What this means for your child is that their genetic inheritance for height won't limit how they enjoy and progress in soccer. It's a sport for everyone to participate in at all levels of the game.

Discovering the world's game

Playing soccer will naturally develop an interest in the wider world of the professional game for any child playing. Kids often want to know who the big stars are, watch and emulate the skills they showcase, and perhaps start following a team as a fan.

This opens a global-sized chance to develop fandom. Soccer has a rich history and an incredible tapestry of teams playing all over the world to discover. It can be a great way for your child to find out a little about global geography — from Madrid to Manchester and beyond. Soccer players come from all countries and continents, representing areas that are less commonly seen in other American sports.

TIP

Following star players is also a great way for your kid to be inspired and look to copy some of the moves and styles of play practiced by the world's top players.

Fortunately, it's now easy in the United States for kids to watch the stars and the action from the world of soccer. Some of the biggest competitions to follow include the FIFA World Cup and FIFA Women's World Cup, both held every four years, along with the top European competitions such as the UEFA Champions League, UEFA Women's Champions League, the English Premier League, and Spain's La Liga, along with the American domestic leagues.

REMEMBER

A lifetime of fun fandom can follow for your kid as they explore the world of soccer, which will further encourage them to play and find out more about tactics and styles of play, informing their own efforts on the field.

Understanding How the Game Is Played

Soccer games are played by two teams on a rectangular field with a goal at each end. The objective for each team is to score goals (points) by getting the ball into the opponent's goal.

Each game is played for an allotted length of time, and the team with the most goals at the end of that time period is the winner. If the teams score the same number of goals in a game, it's considered a tie — or in soccer parlance, a *draw*.

Players in soccer primarily use their feet to strike the ball, with only the goalkeeper permitted to use their hands.

Examining the field of play

At the highest level of soccer, such as a World Cup, soccer is played on a pristine rectangular grass field — often called a "pitch" — measuring between 110 and 120 yards lengthwise and between 70 and 80 yards across. It's just a little larger than an (American) football field. The longer lines on either side of the rectangle are called the *sidelines* while the shorter lines at each end are called the *goal lines* — because centered on this line at either end is the goal.

A goal at either end provides the target for the two teams, consisting of 11 players each, to score in. The goal measures 24 feet wide by 8 feet tall, consisting of two posts and a crossbar connecting them. A net collects the ball struck over the goal line into the goal.

In front of the goal is the *penalty area,* a box measuring 18 yards from each post (see Figure 1-1). This part of the field is particularly important because infringements by the defensive team in this area can result in a penalty kick for the attacking team. (See the "Mastering offside and other key rules" section, later in this chapter, for more information).

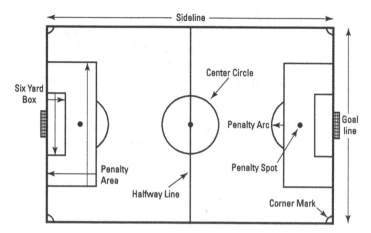

FIGURE 1-1:
The field
of play.

REMEMBER

On your child's journey in soccer, they will play on a vast variety of different sized playing fields, some with natural grass and some with green artificial turf. Full-size fields aren't played on in youth soccer until children are in the over-12 age bracket in most states, because it's far too much space for smaller legs to cover.

Younger kids play on smaller fields with fewer players on each team than at older ages. The size of the pitch and the number of participants increases as age progresses. The size of the goals also changes, from smaller dimensions at younger ages to full-size goals for teenage players.

Roughly speaking, you can likely expect your child to play on the following size fields in these age brackets:

>> **Ages 0–7:** 25–35 yards long and 15–25 yards wide

>> **Ages 8–10:** 55–65 yards long and 35–45 yards wide

>> **Ages 11–12:** 70–80 yards long and 45–55 yards wide

>> **Ages 13+:** 110–120 yards long and 60–80 yards wide

Keeping players and positions straight

Just as the size of the pitch and the dimensions of the goal can vary with the age of those participating, the number of players on the field and the positions they play varies dramatically between younger and older age groups. Children under six play with only two or three teammates, but by the time they've hit the ripe old age of 13, that number will have increased to 11 players on each team.

Though this can vary a bit by local standards, the number of players per team for each age group is roughly as follows:

>> **Ages 0–7:** 3 versus 3, 4 versus 4, or 5 versus 5

>> **Ages 8–9:** 6 versus 6 or 7 versus 7

>> **Ages 10–11:** 9 versus 9

>> **Ages 12+:** 11 versus 11

The positions on the field that players fill can be roughly grouped into four categories. For two of them — *goalkeepers* and *defenders* — the primary aim is to prevent the other team from scoring a goal. (*Note:* The goalkeeper is the only player allowed to use their hands — though only within their own penalty area.) Defenders play in front of the goalkeeper, and are tasked with tackling opponents, intercepting the ball, and passing it to teammates further forward on the field.

REMEMBER

Tackling in soccer isn't the same as tackling in (American) football! You aren't allowed to haul players down with your hands in soccer. Tackling in soccer means using your feet to strip the ball from the opponent's possession — by kicking the ball, not the other player!

Midfielders are typically required to help significantly on both the defensive and offensive aspects of the game, so they need to develop good all-round skills. Players in those positions are particularly relied upon to pass the ball, linking up the play between the defensive and attacking players. And they need to be able to tackle an opponent and intercept the ball to try and stop the opponents from reaching the defensive third of the field.

Attackers are tasked with trying to get the ball into the opponent's net, with the "striker" position aptly named — their role is to strike the ball into the goal.

At the younger ages, particularly for under-sevens, it's worth noting that positions are relatively nominal. Toddlers can't but help to chase the ball, often ending up in a somewhat amusing scrum of kids grouped maniacally around the ball. There also aren't usually dedicated goalkeepers for the small goals pre-schoolers play with.

As kids age up and progress into 6 versus 6 or 7 versus 7 games, some structure starts to develop and goalkeeping is added to the mix. A typical setup in a 6 versus 6 game may see a team have a goalkeeper, two defenders, two midfielders, and one attacker.

Once the game scales up to 9 versus 9, usually at ages 10 to 11, positions become specialized even further. The pitch is now larger, so where players cover the field becomes segmented horizontally across as well as vertically up the pitch. For example, midfielders — the ones who play in the middle of the pitch vertically — will now often be further divided into left, central, and right segments horizontally. Similarly, defenders will cover the center, right, or left of the pitch, also usually in groups of three or four. Attackers, usually numbering only one or two on a team, usually stay fairly central, chasing passes from the players behind them.

As well as location on the field, the role a player has can vary and gets further specialized in older age groups. It is, however, quite simple in the younger age groups. At the under-11 level, the instructions kids are given are usually fairly straightforward to follow — defenders defend, midfielders look to intercept the ball and pass it, and attackers try to score goals.

A good coach will rotate younger players around different positions to ensure that they are learning the game from different perspectives. A defender can learn how to stop an attacker more easily if they have played the position themselves and understand the movements that position requires, for example. It's also fun to try different positions and utilize new skill sets.

At the 9 versus 9 and particularly the 11 versus 11 game sizes, the intricacies of positional play get far more advanced, especially in competitive soccer. It's no longer as simple as a defender defending or an attacker attacking. These more differentiated roles are important to understand so that you know why your kid is playing a specific role, rather than trying to do everything on the field. Some of the most common positions and associated jersey (shirt) numbers are listed in Table 1-1.

TABLE 1-1 **Soccer Positions and Their Associated Jersey Numbers**

Area	Position	Jersey Number	Role
Goalkeeper	Goalkeeper	#1	Stopping the ball from going in the net, typically using the hands.
Defense	Center Back	#4 & #5	Plays in the middle of defense. Usually a strong, taller player and, at older ages, will need to head the ball well.
Defense	Full Back	#2 & #3	Plays wide on the left or right side of defense. Usually a fast player who has the stamina to run up and attack as well as defend well.
Midfield	Holding Midfielder	#6	This player's duty is to shield the play just in front of the defensive line. They are tasked with breaking up opponent's attacks and passing the ball to attacking players.
Midfield	Attacking Midfielder	#8	The playmaker role in soccer is often taken by an attacking midfield player. The aim of this role is to create chances for other players to score goals by providing incisive passes as well as trying to put the ball into the net themselves.
Midfield/ Attack	Winger	#7 or #11	"Wingers" hug the sideline or "wing" of the field, attacking aggressively with speed and dribbling skills. Right footers tend to play right wing and left footers left wing.
Attack	Striker	#9	Goals, goals, goals. The primary job of a striker is to find the back of the net — they spend their time around the opponent's goal looking to shoot.
Attack	Center Forward	#10	While also still looking to score goals, the "number 10" or center forward also plays a role linking the midfield and attack. This is done by looking to pass the ball to other attacking players.

Determining the length of play

Just like the size of the field and the number of players on it, the length of the games your child will play increases as they get older. Typically, the game is also divided into two halves, with a halftime break to allow players to rest. This break is a few minutes for younger players (under the age of 10) and as long as 15 minutes for older players. At younger ages, typically under 8, games are often divided into quarters instead of halves, playing short six- to eight-minute segments with a brief break between each quarter.

As players reach middle school grades, teams start playing halves of 25 minutes each. The game lengths then steadily increase up the years until around the high school age, when a full 45 minutes per half — the same length as a professional match — is reached.

REMEMBER

The clock typically counts *up* in soccer (for example, to 45 minutes) rather than down to zero, so you'll need to remember how long each half is set to be. And at most youth soccer games, up until elite tournament level, you won't see a game clock on the field at all. So if you want to know how long is left in a half, remember to start a timer on your phone or watch to keep check. The referee keeps the official time on their own watch.

TIP

Even when the designated time period is up, extra time is usually added on for stoppages in play (such as injuries or substitutions). The amount of time added is at the referee's calculation and discretion, so you'll never know exactly when a game will end until the whistle peeps three times to signal "full time."

Contemplating the all-important soccer ball

A full-size soccer ball is far too big for a small kid to kick effectively, so it's no surprise that the size and weight of the main object on the field starts smaller and lighter and gets larger and heavier as players age.

In fact, it's very important that kids don't start playing with a ball too large at too young an age. Playing with a smaller ball more suitable to the size of their feet allows kids to develop better skills with the ball. Many of the world's greatest players, such as Lionel Messi, mastered controlling a tennis ball as a child — and this translates into more easily manipulating a larger ball.

So how do you know which size ball your child should play and train with? Balls for outdoor play are grouped into five different sizes by circumference and weight. The smallest is a size 1, which is used by the youngest age groups (under 3) or for technical training at older ages. Size 2 comes into play for toddlers, while size 3 is typically used for beginner youth soccer games at ages 5–8.

Next comes the size 4 ball for 8- to 12-year-olds; it measures 25 to 26 inches in circumference and weighs 11 to 13 ounces. Finally, for teenagers and up into adult games, the size 5 ball comes into play — and your child is now playing with pretty much the same size and weight ball as the top stars at the World Cup. (Table 1-2 summarizes the different ball sizes and weights.)

TABLE 1-2   **Regulation Ball Sizes and Weights**

Ball Size	Ages	Circumference	Weight (ounces)
1	0–2	18"–20"	7–8
2	3–5	23"–24"	10–12
3	6–8	23"–24"	11–12
4	9–12	25"–26"	11–13
5	13+	27"–28"	14–16

Beyond these relatively standardized sized balls for outdoor play, you will also see balls of various other shapes, sizes, and weights. Some are just for fun — how about a glow in the dark ball to play in the dusk in the back yard? Or a soft felt ball so your kid can kick the ball around inside without breaking all the furniture? It's always good to have a variety of balls around the home or in the yard. The more your kid kicks the ball around for fun, the better their foot skills will get.

Some balls have a specific purpose for different formats of the game — a futsal ball (see Chapter 10) has a heavier weight and smaller size to help players keep it under control in a smaller sized field of play, for example.

Fundamentals for Scoring and Stopping Goals

Soccer, as I say earlier, is a simple game to grasp — each team is trying to score a goal, and each team is trying to stop the other from doing so. The skills players need to help their teams score or stop goals can be broken down into a few fundamentals that will be at the heart of all the soccer your child plays growing up.

Here we dive into the basics of each core soccer skill (see Chapter 8 for my perspective on each unique position and skill set):

>> **Dribbling:** Though it has a funny name, running with the ball — keeping it at your feet — is a fundamental core skill when it comes to playing soccer. Little kids naturally want to run with the ball — the harder task is often getting them to pass it! Being able to dribble with the ball at increasing speeds, and using both feet, is a great start to developing good soccer skills.

>> **Tackling:** Approximately half the time, any given team will be defending. Being able to stop an opponent — stripping the ball from them to win possession for their team, or at least blocking the ball to prevent the opponent from moving past them — is a critical skill. Doing so requires stepping in to intercept the ball from an opponent. Players must be careful when tackling — they're not permitted to kick an opponent or haul them down with their arms like in (American) football.

>> **Passing:** However fast any soccer player is at running, they aren't as fast as the ball can move when kicked. This basic truth is why passing is so important and is what makes soccer a team game: The ball can move more quickly from

defense to attack if passed accurately from player to player. Being able to accurately pass and having the vision to know where to pass the ball will make your child a great teammate.

>> **Shooting:** For your team to win, someone needs to put the ball in the back of the net to score a goal. Learning to shoot accurately is a key skill — even better if a player can do so with either the right or left foot, to be able to score from a variety of angles, distances, and opportunities.

>> **Ball control:** Being able to stop the ball and get it under control quickly is a critical skill at any level of soccer. If the ball bounces heavily away off a player's shin or foot, it is likely to go straight to an opponent. Having a good "first touch" — being able to stop the forward momentum of the ball and get it into position to then dribble, pass, or shoot — will position your child to make the right next move with the ball.

REMEMBER

There will never come a time when your child has truly mastered all of these skills. Even a top professional continues to practice and refine all of these elements. But an early focus on the technique needed to be successful in each of these fundamental elements of soccer will pay off in the long run — the ability of children to absorb and learn new skills is stronger at younger ages.

These techniques, the core skills of soccer, are more important to absorb and practice at younger ages than strength or stamina exercises, as those can be supplemented more easily as needed later on. It's much more difficult to learn how to control a soccer ball effectively at older ages, just like learning a language gets harder as we get older.

Mastering offside and other key rules

Soccer may be a simple game to pick up and play, but in organized games there are plenty of rules to get up to speed on to avoid confusion at the peep of a whistle. Most are straightforward to grasp — for instance, unless you're the goalkeeper, don't touch the ball with your hands! — while others are a little more nuanced.

Untangling the offside rule

The offside rule is the trickiest one. Few decisions cause more confusion on the sideline of a youth soccer game than an offside call. This rule won't even be enforced at younger ages because it's difficult for small kids to grasp, but once at the 9 versus 9 level, you'll usually see offside start to be enforced.

The nuance with offside is that the positions of the attacking players, defending players, and the ball itself need to be taken into account. It can be hard from the sideline of a soccer field to even see this accurately, which is why those calls are often controversial.

To boil it down, an attacking player will be penalized for being offside if they are nearer to the opposing goal than both two opponents (including the goalkeeper) *and* the ball when it is played forward to them from a teammate. (See Figure 1-2.) If the ball is played backward to them, a player cannot be offside.

It's important to remember why the offside rule exists. The purpose is to stop attacking players from continually standing next to the goal, which in turn — without an offside rule — would force teams to keep defending deeply to stop balls that are booted up to attackers. The offside rule helps keep the game more balanced and fluid.

REMEMBER

Players cannot be offside when play is restarted on a corner kick, goal kick, or throw-in. Nor can a player be offside when within their own half of the field.

Looking at fouls and penalty kicks

If you hear the referee blow their whistle at a youth soccer match, more likely than not it'll be for an infringement of the rules — an offense by a player that impedes the other team. This may include foul play, such as tripping, kicking, or knocking over an opponent, or striking the ball with the hand (which only the goalkeeper is allowed to do and only inside their own penalty area).

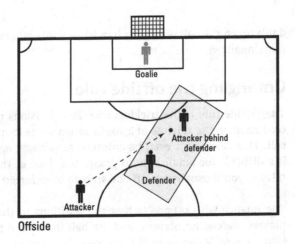

Offside

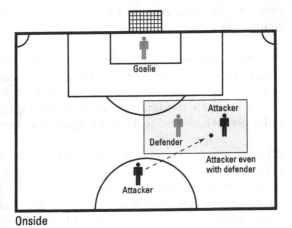

Onside

FIGURE 1-2:
The
offside rule
illustrated.

These types of offenses will result in a *direct free kick* for the opposing team. This means the ball is placed stationary where the offense occurred, and the opposing team has a free kick of the ball — which can be used to pass or shoot directly on goal.

If the offense takes place in the defensive team's penalty area, a penalty kick is awarded to the attacking team — giving them a free shot at goal from 12 yards out (that is the distance on a full-size pitch — it will be marked closer to the goal on smaller-sized youth fields). On the defending team, only the goalkeeper is allowed in the penalty area when a penalty kick is taken, starting on the goal line and attempting to save the shot.

More rarely, *indirect free kicks* are awarded for less serious offenses — such as a pass back from a defender to a goalkeeper that they pick up (the goalie isn't allowed to handle a pass back). It's called indirect because players cannot shoot the ball directly at the goal — it must be passed to a teammate first.

Handing out yellow and red cards

Serious offenses are also subject to further repercussions for the offending player in the form of yellow and red cards.

A yellow card is the lesser of the two cards and is essentially a "caution" (also called a *booking,* because the referee writes the details down in a notebook). Yellow cards are shown for a variety of reasons, including for serious or repeated fouls, time-wasting, or dissent toward the referee. If a player receives a second yellow card, they are then automatically shown a red card and ejected from the game.

A red card can also be shown directly and the player removed immediately from the match if the referee deems a significantly serious offense to have taken place — such as violent conduct toward another player.

In youth soccer, referees won't issue yellow or red cards at the youngest ages. Up to the age of around 10 or 11, although cards may be given out, they are relatively rare and should be used as coaching moments for players to understand that their actions have consequences.

Cards become more frequent at upper middle and high school ages, especially at more competitive levels of play that come closer to senior-level standards. A red card will also result in a player being suspended from playing in the next match as a further punishment.

Dealing with throw-ins, corner kicks, and goal kicks

When the ball goes out of play, the team who last touched it loses possession. The game is restarted by the opposing team. There are multiple ways play is restarted:

>> **If the ball crosses the sideline (the longer lines marking the field), play is restarted with a *throw-in*.** To throw it in, a player places the ball in both hands, holds it behind their head, and then throws it into play from directly above their head. Both feet must be planted down behind the touchline.

Although this technique is not especially difficult, it can be difficult for kids to grasp or remember some of these nuances. It's quite common in youth soccer to see a kind referee coach a youngster who has made a mistake on how to do it correctly — or to see a strict referee pass the ball to the other team!

REMEMBER

The person taking the throw-in cannot throw it to themself. The ball has to be touched by another player first after it is thrown in.

>> **If the ball crosses the line on either side of the goal and is last touched by the defending team, a *corner kick* is awarded to the attacking team.** As the name suggests, this kick is taken from the corner of the field, where the sideline intersects the goal line. This creates a good opportunity from a "set play" — the attacking team will often then cross the ball into the penalty area to try and set up a shot on goal.

>> **If the ball crosses the line on either side of the goal and is last touched by the attacking team, a *goal kick* is taken by the defending team.** The ball has to be kicked from within the 6-yard box that surrounds the goal. This kick is usually, but doesn't have to be, taken by the goalkeeper. They can pass it short or boot it long. The attacking team can't enter the penalty area until the ball is kicked, allowing the defending team to get a clear opportunity for the kick to take place.

When restarting play from a penalty kick, free kick, or corner kick, the player taking the kick can only strike the ball once until another player has touched it. Kicking the ball twice in a row results in a turnover to the other team. This prevents a player from simply dribbling the ball into play.

Handling substitutions

Along with the starters on the field, each team usually has a set of reserve players on the sideline who can be substituted in for another player during the game. At youth level, the number of "subs" usually varies — not every kid on the team roster can make every match, after all. Teams at youth level are usually permitted an unlimited number of substitutions for each match, and players can come in, be subbed out, and return to play later on.

Substitutions take place for a number of reasons, including

>> **Injuries:** If a player receives an injury and can't continue playing or needs a break to recover and be assessed, a replacement player is sent in.

>> **Tactics:** The coach may make a tactical adjustment that requires changing the personnel on the field — for example, if their team is losing, the coach may replace a defensive player with an attacking player to increase the offensive effort.

>> **Playing time:** Particularly in youth soccer and especially so at younger age levels, it's important that every player gets plenty of playing time so they have an opportunity to develop during game play. If your kid is sitting on the sideline every game not playing and not getting subbed in for long, they won't be getting the chance to improve.

>> **Rest:** Soccer, especially if the weather is hot, is a very tiring sport, so it's important for the coach to rotate players and give them a chance to rest on the sidelines and get a drink of water to refresh and be ready to go back in.

In official games, substitutions can only take place when play is stopped and the referee signals to the players that they may enter the field. They should wait for the player they are replacing to reach the sideline before subbing in.

At older levels of play, especially in college soccer, restrictions on the number of substitutes on the sideline and the number of substitutions that can take place come into effect. Your local league will have all the information on what is permitted for substitutions.

Different rules for different ages

Between the ages of 5 and 15, almost everything about the soccer your child plays will change. While the fundamental purpose of kicking a ball into the net to score a goal stays consistent, many of the rules are different for smaller, younger players just getting to know the game at preschool or elementary school age. By the time your kids are teenagers and approaching college, the game looks and follows rules almost identical to adult play.

I explore some of the fundamental differences in the field sizes, ball size, and number of players earlier in this chapter. But there are also some important differences in the way the rules are applied to games for younger players under the age of 10. See the following information for a guide based on official US Youth Soccer rules, though note there may be adjustments in different leagues.

Under 6 (3 versus 3 — no goalkeeper):

>> Games consist of four 8-minute quarters. There's a 2-minute minimum break between the first and second quarters, a 5-minute break between the second and third quarters (halftime) and a 2-minute break between the third and fourth quarters.

>> When the ball goes out of bounds on the sideline, players throw it in. If they do not follow the proper throw-in procedure (see the earlier section "Dealing with throw-ins, corner kicks, and goal kicks"), they are allowed a second attempt.

>> There is no penalty area marked out, and therefore no penalty kicks are awarded for fouls.

>> Infringements lead to free kicks that are indirect (cannot be shot directly at goal, must be passed to another player first).

>> There are no corner kicks — kick-ins or throw-ins are taken instead.

>> An unlimited number of substitutions are allowed, and coaches should make sure players all receive equal playing time.

>> No offside rule is applied.

Under 8 (4 versus 4 — no goalkeeper):

>> Games consist of four 12-minute quarters. There's a 2-minute minimum break between the first and second quarters, a 5-minute break between the second and third quarters (halftime), and a 2-minute break between the third and fourth quarters.

>> When the ball goes out of bounds on the sideline, players throw it in. If they do not follow the proper throw-in procedure (see the earlier section "Dealing with throw-ins, corner kicks, and goal kicks"), they are allowed a second attempt.

>> There is no penalty area marked out and therefore no penalty kicks are awarded for fouls.

>> Infringements lead to free kicks that are indirect (cannot be shot directly at goal, must be passed to another player first).

>> At this age, corner kicks and goal kicks are introduced.

>> An unlimited number of substitutions are allowed, and coaches should make sure players all receive equal playing time.

>> No offside rule is applied.

Under 10 (8 versus 8):

>> At this age, when kids are typically 8 or 9 years old, everything expands quite drastically — from the size of the field, ball, and goals to the number of players, and perhaps most significantly, the addition of goalkeepers. This reflects that a larger goal is now deployed to shoot at.

>> Rather than the quarters used at younger ages, games are now divided into two halves of play like senior soccer matches. The halves last 25 minutes each with a 5-minute break for halftime.

>> When the ball goes out of bounds on the sideline, the standard methods of restart outlined earlier — throw-ins, goal kicks, or corner kicks — are deployed.

>> Penalty areas are now marked out, and penalty kicks are awarded for fouls.

>> Infringements lead to free kicks that can either be indirect or direct — see "Looking at fouls and penalty kicks" earlier in this chapter for an explanation of what this means.

>> An unlimited number of substitutions are allowed, and coaches should make sure players all receive equal playing time.

>> No offside rule is applied.

Once players are past the age of 10, the rules begin to adhere more closely to adult soccer, with the introduction of full-size pitches and goals, offside calls, and longer games that by the time kids become teenagers, largely match the basic rules of the game outlined earlier in the chapter in "Understanding How the Game is Played."

Chapter **2**

Picking the First Places to Play

So, your kid has figured out how to walk — it's almost time for them to start playing soccer! That's right; soccer is such an easy game to play that all your child really needs is enough coordination to kick a ball and they are ready to go.

Programs in most towns and cities start for ages 1 or 2 and up, so you can get your kid out onto the soccer pitch from beginner programs for the littlest ones to recreational teams for elementary and middle school–age kids.

Starter Soccer Programs

Your little one has energy to burn, so it only makes sense to get them out there with other kids on the soccer field. As a sport requiring tons of movement, simply running around playing soccer can get that energy out and allow them to start getting a feel of how to kick the ball while having some fun!

Knowing what to expect

At the very youngest age, most programs for 1- to 3-year-olds aren't something you can just drop off your kid to and then head somewhere else for a coffee or a haircut. In fact, it's often expected and beneficial for parents to be involved on the field with their children at this age.

REMEMBER

Don't worry — you won't be coaching soccer skills! But it is useful for you be around to point your kid in the right direction and reassure them if it's all too much to start with. And no doubt you'll find it fun chasing your toddler and a bunch of soccer balls around!

As well as learning how to kick a soccer ball and receiving instruction on some basic rules (using your feet and not your hands, for example!), your kid's energy will be absorbed by song, dance, and games tangentially related to playing soccer.

Up until the age of 4, sessions are likely to be 30–45 minutes long — anything beyond that would really stretch the attention span of your toddler and your patience as a parent.

At the age of 5 or 6, sessions may last an hour and start to have a bit more structure and focus as attention spans increase slightly among the kids.

REMEMBER

Starter soccer programs aren't about teaching your child how to be a future World Cup winner at the age of 2. Don't expect focused technical soccer skill sessions. They're designed to be fun exercise — with important elements of balance and coordination developing through being out there playing on the field.

TIP

At the age of 2 or 3, there's often a huge divergence in the ability of any child to pay attention to instruction. Your 2-year-old may wander around the field randomly instead of kicking a ball. Don't worry if your child does that, though consider whether you should wait another six months to play if they aren't doing anything there besides picking daisies!

Finding a program

Most big towns or cities have multiple programs available. You can find many with a simple Google search, but it's always a good idea to ask other parents if they know of a good local option. City- or town-run parks and recreation departments often offer beginner soccer programming, and this can frequently be the most cost-effective option.

In addition, multiple national franchises run programs for 2- to 8-year-olds with operations in many states around the country. Signing up for one of these options generally guarantees a good consistency of service provision, curriculum planning, and training for staff. A few of the larger national operations are the American Youth Soccer Organization (AYSO; www.ayso.org), Soccer Shots (www.soccershots.com), and Lil' Kickers (www.lilkickers.com). Check their respective websites to see if they have a program in your area and to see more about the type of classes that each offers.

Your local YMCA also almost certainly runs soccer programming. You probably won't need to be a member to sign up your child, though it'll be more expensive for nonmembers.

Local youth soccer clubs often offer programming for the youngest kids as well as teams for older girls and boys. This can be a good way to get to know a club and see whether it may be a fit for future play when your kid is older.

Here are some things to consider when looking for a program:

>> **Kid to coach ratio:** If you have a child or two of your own, you already know how hard it is to chase them around once they learn to walk. So imagine having a whole bunch of toddlers or preschoolers to corral! Before signing up, ask the program organizer how many kids there will be per coach.

For toddlers, assuming parents will also be supervising their child, anything under a 15:1 ratio of children to coach can work. For preschoolers and above, where parents aren't likely to be holding their child's hand the whole time, you want to see a lower ratio, around 8:1.

>> **Parental expectations:** Make sure you know what you are getting into! As I mention earlier, you can expect your involvement to be required for the youngest kids (1- to 2-year-olds) and continued involvement to be strongly encouraged up to preschool age. Check with the program to find out what they expect of you or whoever accompanies the child to each session.

>> **Fees:** You can likely expect fees to average around $25 per session. Usually, you pay for a multi-month set of sessions upfront, so expect to pay $250 to $350 for 12 weeks of sessions taking place once a week.

>> **Location:** Program locations will vary by what's available in your neighborhood or nearby. In the warmer months, sessions often take place outdoors at a local park. In the colder months, especially in regions with frigid weather, you'll find them at indoor locations such as a local soccer center, YMCA, or public recreation center.

>> **Session length:** Sessions are usually scheduled for the mornings or afternoons. You want to find a location that is convenient for you — there isn't much point traveling half an hour each way to a program that lasts less than an hour.

Getting on a Recreational Team

Toddler and preschool programs are a fun way to introduce your kid to kicking the ball around, but at that age in those types of sessions, it's generally still individualized play. While there may be some efforts to get kids passing the ball to each other, it doesn't get to the heart of what makes soccer so special — learning teamwork.

Understanding the value of playing with others comes through taking the step of joining a team for the first time in a recreational league or program.

"Recreation" is often shortened to "rec," such as in "rec league" or "rec team."

TIP

Don't worry too much about the team your kid joins if they're under the age of 6 — this isn't the time yet to be concerned about the level of play or path for future progression. Getting onto a recreational team is really about your child learning the benefits of sharing the ball and teamwork, the joy of scoring a goal and celebrating with friends, and coming to grips with the rules and how soccer games are played.

Understanding age groups

As of the writing of this book, in most leagues outside of school play, soccer teams are organized by birth year. That means all kids born in, say, 2019 play in leagues with teams whose players were all born in or after that year.

They are designated to this grouping by being *under* a certain age; for example, in 2024 a child born in 2018 would be an *under 6* (abbreviated *U-6*) for games starting play in spring 2024. One year later, that same child would be in the U-7 age category.

REMEMBER

Players can play in older age groups; for example, a child born in 2012 can play up in a 2011 year group. But the reverse isn't true: Players cannot play down in younger age groups.

TIP

This age designation differs from school year grades, which in most states span across two years. Your child may in fact be a young player on their youth soccer team (for example, if they are born in November) while being a relatively older child than most in their school year.

Note: Just as this book was ready to go to press, the authority ultimately responsible for soccer across America — the United States Soccer Federation — ruled that starting in the 2026–2027 season, youth soccer governing bodies will be able to choose between either a birth year or school year age group format. This is a change from the current birth year format, which was first implemented in 2017.

When this new rule comes into place, it will mean flexibility for various leagues to be able to choose whether to organize players by birth year or school year. As governing bodies make these choices, be sure to check the website of the state-level association governing soccer in your region for guidance on how local leagues will be implementing age groupings.

Setting expectations

It's important to start out with realistic expectations for your kid on a team in a recreational league. These are intended to be starter leagues, not for elite development purposes.

REMEMBER

Your child's first team will likely be coached by a parent volunteer — an enthusiast who more likely than not has no professional coaching experience. In fact, that parent coach can be you: When you sign up your child to play, you'll likely be asked if you'd like to volunteer to coach the team. If you do volunteer to coach, head to Chapter 4 to get prepared.

If another parent is in charge, it's important to remember they are a *volunteer*, and they are doing this to help the team. Perhaps they were the only person to raise their hand to fill the role.

The parent isn't likely to have much experience in coaching and may not even be greatly familiar with the sport of soccer. So it's important to support the coach however you can. Don't expect them to be Pep Guardiola (the famous coach of Manchester City) out there.

Understanding seasons

The soccer seasonal year runs similarly to the school year — typically from the start of August one year to the end of July the next year.

Within that seasonal year, leagues are most often organized to play a fall season (usually from August to November) with a winter break to be followed by a spring season (from February to May or June). There's then a summer break to end the year before the cycle begins again!

REMEMBER

These seasons may vary by state or by local league association, so be sure to check the information posted on their respective websites for the calendar of play in your area.

Finding a team

The first step to finding a starter team for your child is to look up a local league. Leagues are organized by various entities. These may include your nearest YMCA, your town or city parks and recreation department, or a local travel youth soccer club under their *recreational* programs.

Unfortunately, there aren't really any comprehensive directories of recreational youth soccer programs available, though your state youth soccer association website may point to affiliated club sites.

TIP

Searching on Google and checking local parks and recreation websites helps locate programs, but be sure to ask other parents whether they know of local leagues. Their firsthand experiences can provide valuable insights.

Registering and paying to play

You will need to sign up your child in advance and register with the league you want to join. This requires providing some basic information about yourself and your child, emergency contact information, and signing various waiver forms.

Payment is usually required at the time of registration. Fees vary widely; for a parks and recreation–run program, a six-game season may cost $50 to $75. A youth soccer club–run program, featuring a couple more games with oversight from dedicated soccer staff, may run $150 to $200.

TIP

Plan ahead to get registered in time — spots can fill up fast, and you don't want to miss out by procrastinating. You can often also save money by signing up sooner rather than later. Many leagues offer "early bird" specials at discounted rates, with fees rising closer to the start date.

Once you've signed up your child, it's time to get the right gear and get set for practices and games. See Chapter 3 for everything you need to know to be ready for your first match day.

Participation expectations

Recreational soccer is an entryway into organized programs for the sport, and the commitments are not too onerous compared to competitive soccer programs for more advanced players (see Part 2).

Here is what you can expect in a rec soccer program — though remember that details vary for each area and league:

>> **Practice:** Usually takes place once or twice per week during the week, typically between 4 p.m. and 7 p.m. Practice often takes place at a local park or youth soccer facility with pop-up smaller goals.

>> **Team size:** Rosters and team sizes vary depending on age — see Chapter 1 for details. Teams at this age usually don't have a designated goalkeeper — the goals are small, and players rotate positions.

>> **Games:** Usually take place on the weekend on either Saturday or Sunday during the daytime. Typically, each game lasts 30 minutes with a short halftime break.

>> **Season:** Games are usually played over a six- to eight-week season. There is often a fall season (starting in September) and a spring season (starting in March). However, you may also be able to find leagues in the winter (indoors if you're in a cold weather climate) or in the summer.

Playing Soccer After School

Signing up your child to play soccer after school in organized programs can serve a number of purposes. Studies have shown that kids participating in any kind of after-school program benefit from periods of increased adult supervision, reducing risky behavior and increasing time spent on productive activities.

In the case of soccer, periods of healthy physical activity are added to your kid's weekly routine; playing can help build confidence; and many programs have a focus on developing important emotional, social, and life skills.

The most straightforward way for your kid to play after-school soccer is if their school offers its own program. That way your child can simply stay and play with no additional transit and either no or a small cost to play. Check to see whether your kid's school offers soccer among its after-school clubs.

TIP

Elementary schools often need parents to volunteer and run after-school soccer programs. You don't need to be a licensed coach or even a soccer expert to help with elementary school soccer. If the reason your kid's school doesn't offer soccer is because they need a volunteer, stick your hand up if you have time to help out.

At older ages in middle and especially high school, soccer programs are more serious and competitive. For all the info on this option, see Chapter 13.

REMEMBER

Many after-school soccer programs are focused on providing the opportunity to play at no cost for diverse and/or underserved groups who may not otherwise have access to "pay-to-play" options.

Examples of programs that serve a larger purpose include

>> **Soccer Without Borders (www.soccerwithoutborders.org):** A nonprofit based in four regions in the United States (California, Colorado, Maryland, and Massachusetts), this program is focused on providing underserved communities — especially immigrants and refugees — the opportunity to play soccer and integrates English-language instruction into many sessions.

>> **Soccer for Success (www.ussoccerfoundation.org):** Run by the US Soccer Foundation, this program provides safe spaces for physical activity, mentorship, and health and wellness development. Its impact includes reducing childhood obesity and encouraging improved nutrition habits, as well as encouraging a love of soccer.

TIP

If your family can benefit from a no-cost after-school program, check out the websites for the previous programs to find out more about availability in your region.

Camping Out with the Soccer Ball

Summertime often means finding ways to keep the kiddos occupied during those vacant days without school. What better option than getting them out on the soccer field with some fun and games for a few hours?

TIP

This section is about camps for your kids just getting started playing soccer at younger ages. For the lowdown on specialized training camps for older and more advanced players, see Chapter 11.

Camps for kids between the ages of 5 and 8 are typically available during the summer holidays. Some camps run all day each weekday for one week, on similar timing to a school day. So you may drop your kiddo off at 9 a.m. and pick them up again at 3 p.m.

Alternately, camps may only be offered for morning or afternoon sessions for a couple of hours. Have a look at what is available in your area and pick something that suits your schedule. At older ages, overnight "sleepaway" soccer camps are also available.

REMEMBER

The camp will require you to prepare your kid for each day's play with the right provisions. This can often mean being asked to pack them plenty of water, a snack, labeled sunscreen, and a packed lunch (if it's an all-day camp). Be sure to check the camp instructions before you send your kid off for their first day.

What to expect at camp

At any good soccer camp, your kid isn't just going to be doing technical passing and shooting drills all day. Especially for the younger age groups, there'll be plenty of fun, games, and prizes given out to keep boredom at bay and engage the kids around soccer-related activities.

Fun games and activities may include

>> Soccer darts

>> Soccer tennis

>> Kickball

Soccer activities on the field may feature

>> Scrimmages

>> Training drills for attacking and defending

>> Individual ball skills

How to find a camp

Similar to finding a starter soccer program or league to play in, locating the right local camp program for your kiddo will most likely come from internet sleuthing or word of mouth.

That said, if you have enrolled your kid in a soccer program or league already, check to see whether the organization running it also offers camp programming. There's a good chance they do, and if so, that can make everything easier: You'll already be registered with them, you should already know a couple of the organizers or coaches, and you'll already be familiar with where their facility is.

Don't overthink it. If you're happy with how the league or program your kid is in is already run, go for the camp with the same organizer.

TIP

If you're starting from scratch, do an internet search for camps in your area. The most cost-effective option may be programs run by your local parks and recreation department. YMCAs are also a good option and usually offer a discount if you're already a member.

Local youth soccer clubs also often provide camps, and attending one of these can be a good way to find out more about a club that may be the next step for your child's play in the future. Local high schools and colleges often offer camps as well.

Registering and paying for camp

Spots in camps are limited, so be sure to search for and sign up early — try to secure a spot a couple of months before the camp or you may miss out. Camps have a deadline listed to enroll by, but they can also fill up before that date, so don't leave it until the last minute.

Registration for camps is now done online for most programs. You'll likely need to provide some basic information about your child, sign various participation waivers, and pay the required fee.

Camp fees vary vastly depending on the number of days, amount of time per day and level of the camp. For a typical week of half-day or full-day camp at the U-8 age or below, expect to pay around $150 to $300.

Chapter **3**

Going to the First Game

Your little tyke has their soccer jersey on, a ball at their feet, and it's time to play a game! It all sounds so simple, but some basic preparation can help ensure that when the game kicks off, your kid has everything they need, and you're all set on the sidelines.

Wearing the Right Stuff

Getting out onto the soccer pitch doesn't require an extensive amount of equipment, but there are some key soccer-specific items you'll need to get ready for your child's first match.

The soccer *uniform* is named as such because, like in most team sports, the team should be uniformly dressed the same. That means if your team is designated to wear blue shorts, your child should wear blue shorts — this isn't the moment to express individuality by wearing green shorts!

The uniform (also called a "kit") consists of three main articles of clothing:

>> **Jerseys:** Also called "shirts," jerseys are the main element of the team uniform. Jerseys are usually short-sleeved, though long-sleeved one are permitted. They're typically made of a polyester material that's lightweight, breathable, and stretchable. Jerseys generally feature a primary color, sometimes along with a complementary accent color.

>> **Shorts:** Apart from the goalkeeper, all players always wear shorts — however cold it is outside! (See the later section "Grabbing Additional Gear" for options to help stay warm in colder conditions.) Players on the same team wear matching shorts. These aren't always the same color as the jersey or socks but are designed to follow the style of the uniform as a whole. They can feature the team logo or just be a plain single color.

>> **Socks:** Soccer socks are made of thick synthetic fiber materials, such as spandex and polyester. The socks are long, stretching up to just short of the knee, in order to accommodate the shin guards your kid will wear underneath (see more on shin guards in "Grabbing Additional Gear"). Like the jersey and shorts, the color is coordinated to be part of the overall uniform look.

REMEMBER

Your team may well have both a *primary* and *secondary* uniform, also known as a *home* and *away* uniform. This is to try to ensure that the two teams on the field don't wear the same colors — for example, if Team A has a red primary uniform jersey color and Team B also has a red primary jersey, one of the teams will instead wear their secondary uniform (perhaps a blue jersey). Otherwise, it would be hard for the players and especially the referee to identify who is on which team. When you sign up your child for a team, the administrators will let you know what color combinations to wear for each match.

TIP

The saying goes that "goalkeepers are different," and this is reflected in the uniform they play in as well. If your kid is minding the net, visit Chapter 8 for info on what goalkeepers must wear.

Sizing Up Shoes

No other piece of equipment is as important to the soccer player than what's on their feet. After all, the purpose of the sport is to kick the ball!

Soccer shoes are known as *cleats* (or "boots" if you go across the Atlantic to England), and there's a wide variety to choose from at online retailers or your local sporting goods or specialized soccer store. Read on for a guide on what to look for.

Getting the right fit

Ill-fitting soccer shoes are a recipe for a fiasco on the soccer field. If they're too tight, they'll be uncomfortable and lead to blisters. If they're too loose, they'll flap around, making it hard to run properly and kick the ball cleanly. Some shoes are narrower than others, and the same is true for your child's feet — every foot and every make of shoe is a little different, so it's critical to find the right fit.

TIP

You're aiming for comfort and a snug, but not too snug, fit. As a general rule, there shouldn't be a gap at the heel and there should be a small gap (around the size of your child's thumb) between the big toe and the front of the shoe.

REMEMBER

The size shoe your child wears for their regular shoes is likely to be roughly the right size for soccer shoes, but don't assume it translates perfectly and just order the same size shoe online. It's important to measure or try on soccer shoes to get the right fit, especially as each manufacturer has slightly different sizing.

The best way to ensure a good fit is to go to a specialist soccer store, if one is close enough to you, or a sporting goods store. There, your child can try on a number of options, and you should be able to get good advice on the right fit from the clerk. It's important to wear actual soccer socks when going to the store to try on shoes. This helps you get the right fit.

TIP

When sizing up shoes, leave a little room for growth so you're not buying a new set of expensive cleats in only a few weeks.

Selecting shoes for starting out

Particularly at younger ages just starting out in preschool soccer, the only thing to really worry about when purchasing shoes is a good fit.

Picking an elite brand, a particular style, or considering any so-called performance benefits from a major manufacturer aren't going to matter to the child or impact how they learn the game at this age.

Under the age of 6, it's all about finding a comfortable fit so their first experiences out on the soccer field aren't negatively impacted by any discomfort they may not even be able to articulate.

TIP

Pick a color for the cleats that your kid likes — it'll make playing in them a bit more fun and exciting!

Cleats for older and advanced players

As your child gets older and potentially starts to play more competitive soccer, you'll have good reasons to pay attention to the materials and features different types of shoes offer.

The type of footwear your child needs depends on the surface that they are playing on. Some surfaces require more grip with studded soles, while others (such as gym floors) need to have flat bottoms. Here's a guide to the type of surface and the terminology for the soccer shoe you'll need to find:

>> **Grass:** Your child will spend most of their soccer-playing life on grass, as it's the original and most ubiquitous surface for organized games and practices. For this surface, your kid needs cleats with studs that dig into and grip the ground.

 The studs are either bladed or conical (round) and are often called "firm ground" cleats by manufacturers.

>> **Artificial turf:** A lot of soccer is now played on artificial turf, which has a harder surface than grass with thinner

turf. Shoes made for this surface have more studs than grass cleats to provide good grip, but the studs are much shorter as they don't need to dig into the ground as deeply.

It's a good idea to get a pair of this type of shoe if your kid will play on artificial turf. Wearing grass cleats on artificial turf can be uncomfortable on the joints.

>> **Indoor/gym:** An increasing amount of soccer is now played indoors on gym floors, especially the small-sided game of *futsal* (see Chapter 10). Soccer shoes for indoor play and futsal should have flat soles made of rubber to grip the flat gym surface.

This type of shoe is typically lightweight and very similar to many regular types of tennis shoes. In fact, in a pinch your kid can wear flat-soled sneakers when getting started playing indoors.

REMEMBER

Much like sneakers, there's a lot of marketing around the style and various promised performance benefits of more expensive soccer shoes from manufacturers such as Nike, Adidas, and Puma. At the end of the day, a good fit and durable material are more important than bells and whistles promised with marketing buzzwords.

KNOWING WHEN IT'S TIME FOR NEW SHOES

Getting a new pair of cleats is an expensive purchase, and there's no need to do it each season just for the sake of it. Instead, consider the following factors to determine when it's time for a pair of new kicks:

- **Sized out:** Perhaps the most obvious reason for new shoes is when they are fitting too tightly. Maybe your child has a younger sibling they can be passed on to!

- **Lacking traction:** The actual cleats (studs on the bottom of the shoe) will eventually wear down, particularly if your child is

(continued)

(continued)

playing a lot on artificial turf. This can lead to a lack of traction, making it hard to turn effectively, and can result in your child slipping on the field. Check the bottom of the cleats periodically to see if some of the studs are getting worn away.

- **Distressed condition:** If the upper body of the shoe starts falling apart or the inner lining is worn out, performance and comfort will start to be negatively impacted.

Grabbing Additional Gear

Along with a uniform and cleats, there are several other items you'll definitely need as well as some optional items that may help your kid stay more comfortable out there on the pitch, especially in colder weather conditions.

Soccer ball

You can determine the right size ball to get from Table 1-2 in Chapter 1, but you'll quickly find yourself overwhelmed by the bewildering array of options at your local sports equipment retailer or online store.

REMEMBER

Your child certainly doesn't "need" the most expensive option: These are typically official balls that replicate those played with in the top tournaments, such as the FIFA World Cup. These can retail for as much as $170. While this may make for a nice (expensive) birthday gift, you're really paying for the branding versus the quality of the ball itself. If you just want a good ball for your kid to play with, you should be able to find a high-quality product for around $50 and serviceable options for half that. Beware of very cheap balls that may not last much longer than a few good kicks.

Shin guards

Ever been kicked on the shin? It hurts! And at the high velocity of a foot swinging to try and kick the ball, an unprotected shin can be seriously injured. That's the reason all organized soccer games require *shin guards* (also known as shin pads). And, really, it's a good idea to have your kid wear them anytime they play.

Shin guards won't come with any team uniform purchase, so you'll need to purchase these via an online retailer or at a sporting goods store. Make sure to check the sizing — adult shin guards will be far too large for junior legs, so order something marked at the appropriate age for your child.

The simplest type of shin guard simply slips down the front of the player's sock. It is made of hard plastic on the front to reduce the impact of anything striking the shin and a soft pad on the back to comfortably lay on the front of the shin, curved slightly to match the contour of the leg.

Some shin pads have a Velcro strap that wraps around the back of the leg to keep them in place or a sleeve that is placed around the leg for the guard to be tucked into.

TIP

More elaborate shin guards may also include ankle protectors. These can be a bit bulky but provide more protection.

Cold weather gear

A long-sleeve base layer can add a lot of warmth to the core body temperature when playing in colder weather. The color should match that of the team jersey in official matches. These should be made of polyester, moisture-wicking material for maximum comfort.

Compression shorts or leggings can also be worn under team shorts on days where the chill will really be felt.

TIP

Goalkeepers will be wearing them already, but there's no rule against outfield players wearing gloves to keep warm when needed. Bulky gloves are awkward to run around in, so you want a tight-fitting, sleek style for your kid to wear.

Headgear

For goalkeepers, a baseball cap can be a great addition to help shield the eyes from the sun. Outfield players aren't technically allowed to wear caps or hats, though at the youth level (and particularly in recreational soccer), some leniency is usually shown, especially in cold weather. Beanies can be worn during training if coaches allow due to cold weather.

Players with long hair should wear headbands or hair ties to keep hair out of their eyes, which can impede vision by flapping around the face during play.

Water bottle

Staying hydrated is a necessity when playing soccer. It's worth investing in a good, durable water bottle with a large capacity — at least 32 ounces but ideally 64 ounces. Vacuum-insulated bottles can keep water colder longer, though filling a large jug bottle with plenty of ice can also do the trick.

Soccer bag

All this gear needs to be organized when headed to the soccer field. At a minimum, you need a place to keep the cleats, shin guards, water bottle, and ball. Purchase a simple soccer backpack for your kid to transport all of this.

In competitive soccer, purchasing a branded team backpack may be part of the required equipment each season, but for recreational play you can pick up a solid backpack for around $30 to $40 at an online retailer or local sporting goods store.

Getting Set on the Sideline

Right, you've learned the basics of the game, got your kid out and about kicking the ball for fun, signed them up for a rec team, and navigated getting their uniforms and equipment set.

Now it's time to get yourself set on the sidelines — if your kid ends up loving the game, you'll spend an incredible amount of time watching them play (and playing taxi driver), so settle in and read on to do it right!

Arriving on time

First things first: You need to know the address of the soccer complex or park and the field your child will be playing at. Have a look at the complex on Google or Apple Maps to get the lay of the land.

To help you find the right pitch to play on, fields are usually assigned a number or letter. At the younger ages (4–8 years old), the fields are small and close together. At older ages (over 9), the fields become larger, more spread out, and harder to find.

TIP

The key, though, is to give yourself extra time to get there and get set, especially for the first game. Not only will the field be unfamiliar but so will the experience and the setting for your child and yourself.

You'll probably be asked to arrive at the field 15 or 30 minutes before game time — build in an extra 10 minutes on top of that in case of any traffic delays, parking challenges, or time spent locating the field to ensure that you're there comfortably on time. It's better to be early and get your kid set to play calmly rather than rushing around at arrival.

Getting comfortable

For most of your child's soccer life, until they reach the giddy heights of high school or college soccer playing in proper stadiums, you need to remember one important thing — bring your own chair! Very rarely is seating provided at youth soccer fields.

REMEMBER

Bring a lawn or camping chair that's comfortable enough to sit in for an hour or so but not too heavy to carry, as you may find yourself trekking across a few soccer fields to get to where your kid is playing.

TIP

Some chairs even come with attached sun umbrellas for some shade!

Once you're there, locate the parents from the kids on your child's team. You'll usually sit together as a group, and this provides a great chance to get to know the other parents. You can exchange tips and thoughts about soccer (or anything else!) and even arrange carpools (see Chapter 6 for a deep dive into excelling at logistics).

While you've certainly made sure your child has adequate water and sunscreen, have you prepared yourself? On a hot day, sitting on the sideline can also be a thirsty and baking day, so be prepared with both for yourself and any of your child's siblings watching alongside.

Having the right expectations

Settle down in your lawn chair and cheer on your child! Yes, it's really that simple. You're not on the sidelines to coach the team, to chastise the referee, or in fact to do anything else. Positive reinforcement is what your kid needs to hear — anything else is just added noise that can often negatively impact the experience for everyone.

REMEMBER

Particularly at younger ages, it's also important not to worry very much about the scoreline. Of course, it's nice for your kid to win their games. But losing — and learning from it — is also an important part of the experience of growing up. The scores in recreational soccer games aren't important in the long run. You want to focus on your kid having fun.

TIP

If you're stressed out on the sidelines about the score, or the referee, or the coach, that's likely to be picked up by your kid and make their experience less enjoyable.

So sit back in your lawn chair, support your kid, and enjoy the game. For more on how to behave on the sidelines, especially as your child potentially joins more competitive programs in older age groups, see Chapter 5.

Chapter **4**

Parent Coaching and Refereeing

ecreational soccer is a relatively low-cost activity run for the fun and enjoyment of kids playing. Part of the reason costs can be kept low, versus the much higher fees of competitive levels of soccer, is due to the time contributed by parents and others to volunteer key services such as coaching or refereeing.

If you want to find out more about helping out and being more involved with your child's soccer, read on!

Volunteering to Help Out

Every team needs a coach, but at the recreational soccer level, most teams — especially at younger ages — won't have a specialized professional. It's often a volunteer parent, so it could be you!

You may not have expected to volunteer as a parent-coach when you signed your kid up to play soccer, but someone had to stick their hand up, and there's no better person than you, after all.

Even if you've never played or even watched much soccer before, you can be a successful parent-coach and ensure that the kids enjoy playing — which is the goal.

There's a wide range in the extent of preparation that leagues or clubs offer volunteer coaches. At the youngest age, coaching toddlers, you may just be thrown in at the deep end without any training. Some leagues or programs may provide lesson plans outlining drills you can use each week of the season.

In some programs, though, not only will training be offered — it'll be required. For example, the American Youth Soccer Organization (AYSO), which is one of the largest nationwide youth soccer groups, requires parent volunteer coaches to take courses that provide basic certification as well as agree to a background check. This includes taking a "Safe Haven" class online or in-person, which includes training on safety protocols along with age-specific coaching courses. These courses can take several hours to complete.

If you're interested in taking further coaching education training, check out the information about "Grassroots Coaching" at the United States Soccer Federation website, www.ussoccer.com.

Every rec program varies, but here are a few fundamentals to remember as you get ready to start coaching kids:

>> **Have a plan.** Small kids are easily distracted and a whole group of them can be a recipe for disorganized chaos if you don't know what you're planning to do next in any training session or in getting them ready before a game. This chapter gives you lots of ideas on drills and warm-ups to have planned out for each session.

>> **Make it fun!** No kid will remember the score of a soccer game between two teams of 8-year-olds in the years to come, but they will remember if they had fun — and stayed on the journey playing soccer. Enjoy the time spent with the kids and they will enjoy it as well. Focus on the joy of playing together rather than the score.

>> **Be positive.** Coaching can be frustrating if kids aren't listening or are struggling on the pitch, but this is when it's even more important to stay positive. Your good energy will be followed by the kids. Singling out kids for negative feedback or shouting at them during games will only backfire.

>> **Ask for help.** Don't coach alone! Just because you were the parent who raised their hand to lead the effort doesn't mean others shouldn't or wouldn't help out. Ask if someone will volunteer to be an assistant to help organize, cover a training session if you can't make it for some reason, and be a person you can bounce ideas and thoughts off. Other parents will be grateful for your contribution, and many may be glad to step up and support.

Preparing for the Season

Getting ready for the season means making sure you have a plan in place for both practice sessions and games. This section guides you through the equipment you'll need to run your first practice and how to ensure that the team is ready to go — and on time! — for the first game day.

REMEMBER

No one is going to expect you to transform your team of beginners into World Cup winners. Nor should you expect every practice to run to military precision or to win every game. In fact, it's not about winning or being perfect in practice — it's about providing a safe, engaging atmosphere for your kids. So one of the best ways to prepare for the season is to set your own expectations about making it enjoyable for the kids and accepting that working with a bunch of young girls or boys brings a bit of chaos at times!

Equipment

Fortunately, soccer is a simple game that doesn't need a massive amount of equipment to play or coach. There are, though, a few things you'll need to run drills effectively:

>> **Soccer balls:** This one might be obvious, but of course it wouldn't be much of a soccer practice without soccer balls.

Having a bag of balls, properly inflated, is the starting point for any practice. You can also ask kids to bring their own ball to practice. Make sure you have the appropriate size balls for the age group you are coaching (see Table 1-2 in Chapter 1 for a guide).

TIP

Be sure to have a soccer ball pump and needle on hand at every practice. Underinflated balls are no fun to play with!

>> **Pinnies:** Also called "bibs," these lightweight mesh vests come in various colors and are used to identify players on teams or during drills. These will need to be washed between practices to avoid a funky stink developing!

>> **Cones:** Small cones are used for multiple reasons in training drills, from simply marking off zones to play in to arranging in different ways for advanced challenges and drills. Typically 2 inches tall and 7 inches wide, they are compact and easy to transport. Cones usually come in packs of 25 or 50 cones each.

>> **Soccer goals:** You won't be playing in full-size goals on existing soccer fields with players under the age of 10. Those goals would be much too big. Instead, you'll need small pop-up goals that can be placed wherever you need them on the field.

REMEMBER

The league or club you are volunteer coaching for should provide all of the preceding equipment for you, and information about it should be shared as you are onboarded to coach.

Communication with parents

Before the first practice or game, send a note via email to parents introducing yourself, explaining the expectations for the season, and asking for help where you need it. This sets you and the team up for a smoother season.

Here are a few things you may want to go over in your introductory note:

>> **Your bio:** This doesn't need to be your whole life story, but it's nice for the other parents to know who you are, which

child is yours, if they have other siblings, and a couple of other details.

>> **Your soccer knowledge:** It's okay if you don't have any! You've volunteered for this role, and it's good for parents to know if you're new to the sport, have a little knowledge, or are a qualified soccer coach. It'll help set the right expectations and tone for the season.

>> **Group communication:** How do you plan to communicate with other parents on things like practice and game times, or other important logistical information? How can they contact you with questions or to let you know about whether their child can make it to a game? This is the time to let them know whether to expect emails, group texts, or if there is a parent portal set up by the league that you'll be communicating through.

Getting some assistance

You can't do this alone! Hopefully, during the same process by which you volunteered to become the coach, an assistant from the parent pool was also recruited to support you. If not, reach out to the other parents and see if someone will volunteer for the role.

TIP

An assistant coach supports the head coach at practices and games, aids in logistics, and helps in communicating with parents and players. If the lead coach is not available to run a practice session or game for some reason, the assistant steps in and takes charge. Assistant coaches, along with the head coach, help to foster a positive and fun environment around the team.

Mastering Coaching Fundamentals

The aim of coaches is to get the team organized and lead a fun, positive experience on the soccer field. Building bonds of teamwork and togetherness that apply beyond the soccer field gives everyone a productive experience.

That said, it's certainly helpful to comprehend the basics of soccer, have a few drills in your practice plan, and understand how to manage at game time. See Chapter 1 to make sure you're up to speed on the rules of the game and read on for some coaching tips to start harnessing your inner Ted Lasso.

Simple drills to get kids playing

Your practice session will last 45 minutes to an hour depending on the age of your kids (shorter for under sixes, longer for under eights). Each practice can be broken down into a handful of segments with a couple of drills in each and water breaks in between:

>> Warm-ups

>> Fun soccer drills

>> Small-sided scrimmage

The key with younger kids is to keep them moving and keep boredom and distraction at bay — this means fun, active, and short drills. Following are some ideas on how to run each section of your practice.

REMEMBER

Kids under the age of 10, especially in group situations, don't have the patience for long explanations or lectures. Remind them at the start of your first practice that you are all there to have fun, respect each other, and listen so that everyone can enjoy it more. If you need to explain something, keep it short and sharp: You probably have 10–15 seconds until you rapidly lose the attention of the child or group.

Consider "gamifying" practice by rewarding players with points for certain achievements, as this can encourage more enthusiastic participation among kids.

Warming up

Young children's muscles — still the model of elasticity — don't need as much warming up as those of older kids and adults. There's no need to do a bunch of static stretches that are difficult for small kids to focus on. Instead, you can start each session with some basic movement through some fun games. This helps focus their attention, gets them moving, and develops good balance and body control.

Dynamic activities to kick off a warm up can be as simple as side shuffles, back peddling, or jumping jacks.

The following sections get you up to speed on a few simple warm-up drills.

Traffic Lights

Green means go, yellow means slow, and red means stop — this drill is as easy as a traffic light! Set up your kids in a designated zone (marked by cones) large enough for them all to run around dribbling the ball (kicking it to themselves).

Call out "green light" for go and your players should start dribbling the ball quickly with small touches. Call out "yellow light" and they should continue dribbling, but slowly. Now shout out "red light" and they should try and stop the ball with their foot as fast as possible and freeze. Restart with a yellow or green light and continue on for a few minutes!

TIP

You can add lots of variations to this drill to keep it interesting in different sessions. For example, ask the kids to dribble with only their right or their left foot. Or add another color to the mix that can add some fun — perhaps purple means sitting on the ball! You can even ask the kids themselves to nominate a color with a different variation.

Sharks and Minnows

Your kids may be familiar with this one already from other activities, but it's a fun one with a soccer ball added to the mix, getting the whole team moving.

Mark out an area roughly 20-x-20 feet (it may be larger or smaller depending on how many kids are participating). Each "minnow" is a player dribbling a ball, and they start on one side of the zone. The "sharks" (at least two of them) do not have a ball and start in the middle.

The minnows aim to dribble the ball across the zone to the other side (and back again) without the sharks intercepting the ball and kicking it out of the zone. If this happens, the minnow becomes a shark — and the game becomes harder for all the remaining minnows. The last remaining minnow wins!

TIP

An easy bit of good technical advice to teach is to remind the minnows to keep the ball close to them when they are dribbling it by taking small touches so that they are controlling the ball and keeping it away from sharks. The same principle will apply in real games of soccer!

The Name Game

Most your players may not know each other's names, so this drill can either be used to help them learn them or just to have them start thinking ahead when passing the ball.

Have your team form a circle. One player starts with one ball and passes it to another player. That player must shout out the name of the next player they will pass to while receiving the ball, and then kick it to that player. They should take a touch to get the ball under their control, and then play their pass.

TIP

Add a second ball toward the end of the drill for some added fun!

Drilling soccer fundamentals

After the warm-ups and a quick sip of water, it's time for a couple of more drills that are slightly more focused on teaching some of the technical fundamentals of soccer, though the aim is still to keep things simple, engaging, and active.

Pick one or two drills (or a similar drill that you can find online) from the following sections for each session and rotate them each week. Don't try to pack too many drills into one session or spend too long trying to explain the purpose of the exercise. The drill itself should be a fun teacher.

TIP

You can find dozens more drills online by Googling for soccer drills for the age group you are coaching. Websites such as www.soccerdrive.com or www.soccerxpert.com also list dozens of drills. Make sure whatever drills you run, the kids are moving as much as possible and not waiting in lines to kick the ball, which is when boredom and distraction can set in.

Dribbling

For younger kids in particular, keeping the ball at their feet is often the easiest way to keep them focused — and all those touches of the ball help develop one of the most fundamental parts of good soccer technique — being comfortable in possession of the ball. So be sure to keep a solid rotation of dribbling drills in your sessions, such as freeze tag. Everyone knows how to play tag, so this is an easy one to get kids running around (with the ball) trying to evade the tagger.

Set up a square measuring around 15-x-15 feet with cones. All kids should start inside the square with a ball at their feet. Now it's time for them to evade the tagger on your signal! You can either nominate a kid to be the tagger or do it yourself if you want a bit of exercise.

When a player is tagged, they need to freeze in place and do toe taps on the ball (lightly stepping on the top of the ball with their toes) for 30 seconds. After that, they can start moving again.

Play in one-minute increments, rotating the taggers. Through the familiar fun of tag, this drill helps develop a key core soccer skill of spotting the tagger with peripheral vision and turning quickly with the ball to evade them.

Passing

Young soccer players tend to chase and herd around the ball. Once they get it, they typically don't want to give up possession. But passing is fundamental to soccer, so here are a couple of activities that can help impart some of the basics and benefits of teamwork and passing:

>> **Triangles:** Set up a large rectangular area (approximately 25-x-30 feet) and place three cones inside to form a small triangle, spacing them about 3 feet apart. Now place another six sets of triangles randomly within the rectangle area.

Separate your group into pairs with one ball each. Their goal is to pass the ball to each other through each triangle. If you want to gamify it, have each team score a point for each triangle pass and see how many they can make in three minutes. This teaches taking advantage of partnership to succeed and keeps the kids moving while passing!

>> **Rondo:** This classic passing drill is easy to set up and is essentially soccer's version of monkey in the middle.

Set up a square with cones spaced 15 or 20 feet apart. Two players will be in the middle, and the remainder (ideally four to six) on the outside. One player starts with the ball, and they are trying to retain possession among the "outside" players while the "inside" players try to intercept the ball. An "outside" player who loses the ball to an "inside" player or kicks it out of the square swaps places with an inside player.

This drill is easy to understand, has a spirited competitive element to it (to keep the ball), and subtly teaches important fundamental soccer skills: passing the ball quickly, thinking ahead, and keeping possession for your team.

Shooting

Kids usually love shooting the ball. The challenge here is finding drills that keep everyone moving and getting enough shots at a target — and making sure the kids are collecting balls from wayward kicks as they go! "Hit the coach" is one such drill that's fun as long as you can shout OUCH loud enough to entertain the kids!

Shooting is all about striking the ball well and toward a target accurately. The entertaining twist in this game is that you and your assistant coaches are the targets — and what kid wouldn't love the chance to kick a ball at an adult?

Set up a 15-x-15-foot square with cones and make sure every kid has a ball. Then walk or jog (depending on how often the kids are accurately hitting you) and ask your players to hit you with the ball.

Every strike on target should come with a loud OUCH from you or your assistant and earns a point for the kicker. Do this for 5–10 minutes — or until you get sick of getting hit by the ball!

Young kids aren't always the best at following instruction — as a parent, you likely already know this. If several kids aren't following the drill, pause and make sure they aren't confused about what to do. If the kids are still acting up and being goofy, remind them that they are here to practice and it's not fair on the team if everyone doesn't participate.

Scrimmaging to end the session

After trying to herd kids to follow drills for the majority of your practice session, you'll be relieved that it can be closed out with a simple and much-loved scrimmage game.

Scrimmages simulate the setup of a real game, giving players experience in the situations they will face and the opportunity to work on teamwork and try out some of the skills they have been learning.

Setting up a scrimmage means dividing your players up into two teams. Based on your knowledge of the varied skill levels of the kids, try to make the teams fairly even in terms of ability if you can. Give each team a different colored pinny so players can identify their teammates.

Set up a field the appropriate size for your group with a goal at either end. You can mark out sidelines and end lines for out of bounds by placing cones at intervals to form a rectangle. Recommended field sizes for scrimmages are as follows:

>> 3 versus 3: 25 yards long by 15 yards

>> 4 versus 4: 30 yards x 20 yards

>> 5 versus 5: 35 yards x 25 yards

>> 6 versus 6: 45 yards x 30 yards

>> 7 versus 7: 55 yards x 40 yards

If you have an uneven number of players for each team (which will happen if you have an odd number of players at practice), you can designate one player as an "all-time attacker." They should be given a different colored pinny than the two teams. Their job is always to help whichever team has possession of the ball score a goal — they do not defend.

A scrimmage is a chance to let the players experience a game situation and figure out for themselves how to play as a team. Only interrupt play if you need to — if a child is being disruptive, for example — so the kids can get a feel for being out there and working out game situations on their own.

Dealing with disruption

Recreational soccer practice shouldn't feel like a military boot camp, and if you've followed the advice offered here to keep practice fun and engaging, hopefully most of the kids are following along most of the time.

As we all know, though, take any group of ten kids and the odds are one or two may be — how do we put it kindly? — slightly less obedient than others.

In addition, some kids — especially at the preschool age — struggle with attention span and may wander off or struggle to pay attention.

The way to handle this depends on the age of the kids.

Kids under the age of 5 or 6 are prone to distraction, and as a coach of their soccer team for an hour or two a week, you're not going to change that dramatically. At that age, the best thing to do with a child struggling to follow along or pay attention is to try and gently steer them back. Pairing them with another child who is following along can be helpful.

For older kids, aged seven and up, it's important to set up expectations from the first practice and consistently stick to the rules around behavior throughout the season.

Some of the expectations you'll want to convey to all the players at the start of the first practice are

>> Follow directions from the coach at all times.

>> Listen when the coach is talking and do not talk over others.

>> Be kind to your teammates and do not be mean.

TIP

Ask the kids themselves to suggest which rules should be followed. If they can buy into the idea that everyone should follow along and be good teammates, you're in a positive starting position.

What should you do if a player isn't following rules and is disrupting practice?

Start with a simple reminder of the expectations and rules, explaining why it's important for the team. If the disruption continues, put the player on a timeout, explain the reasoning again, and determine when they can return to play (two or five minutes are reasonable intervals).

If you continue to have problems with a child's disruptive behavior, it's time to have a conversation with their parents as the root cause may well be something only they can tackle versus their volunteer soccer coach.

WARNING

Running laps or doing push-ups as a form of punishment is counterproductive — this associates physical fitness drills with negativity and can lead to feelings of animosity.

Setting up team formations

Players line up on the field in specific formations that designate roles for each player (see Chapter 1 for more on different roles). At the professional level, these formations are complex arrangements of 11 players — fortunately for coaching recreational youth soccer, it's an awful lot simpler!

Ages 0–6

For young kids under the age of seven, the number of players on one team — between three and five — means positioning and formations are very simple. There's no goalkeeper playing at this age, remember.

You also can't expect a 4-year-old to stick closely to positional instruction — at that age, almost every kid on the field will simply be chasing the ball wherever it goes! So don't worry too much about positions at this stage.

You can designate a couple of players as defenders and a couple as attackers. The defenders will line up and try to stay farther back on the field, stopping goals, while the attackers will be further forward, looking to dribble and shoot on goal.

Ages 7–9

At ages 7 to 9, the number of players usually expands to seven per team, which does necessitate some positioning so that players have roles and space out from each other. That said, there is no point trying to overcomplicate it, and players should switch and rotate during games.

You'll also be adding a goalkeeper to the mix at this age. You may or may not have a kid or two on your roster who actively want to play in goal. If you don't, the fairest solution is to rotate the position among the players. This is easiest to do by switching the goalkeeper at halftime each game and having different players in the role over multiple games.

The other six players will be positioned across defense, midfield, and attack. You'll want to have at least two defenders and two midfielders as these are key areas to have multiple players covering. You can then either play with two attacking forwards or just one attacker, and reinforce the midfield or defense with one more player. Experiment and see what works for your team.

Managing games to keep it fun

Game day is coming! It can be a little intimidating showing up for the first match and knowing you are responsible for getting the kids out onto the field and organized during the game. But don't worry too much — follow these tips and you'll have your kids out there and enjoying the match in no time.

Before the game

There are a few things to remind parents of via your group communication tool prior to the first game of the season:

>> **Equipment:** Remind parents that kids *must* wear shin guards, and to bring plenty of water and a ball (for warm-ups) to the game.

>> **Arrival location and time:** Be clear on where parents need to go (providing the facility location address and field number) and when you expect them to arrive. Thirty minutes before the kickoff time will give everyone a bit of buffer time and the opportunity for warm-ups before the game.

At the game

Once you're at the field getting ready for kickoff, be sure you have a plan for the game ahead:

>> **Warm-ups:** As kids start to arrive, check to see that they have shin guards on and then send them out on the field for warm-ups. Ideally, your assistant coach can help with this. You can use a couple of the simple drills listed earlier to get them moving.

>> **Pre-match huddle:** Get the kids together in a group circle. Remind them to have fun and be good teammates. Explain the (simple) formation you'll be playing and who will be playing where. End with a group team cheer.

>> **Rotate players:** Everyone should receive equal playing time, so be ready to swap players in during a break in play. Players should rotate positions as well to try different roles — for example, a defender in the first half should switch to an attacking position in the second.

>> **Provide encouragement:** Offer positive reinforcement and energetic support to your players from the sideline. Trying to point out mistakes or provide coaching points during the run of play is likely to be counterproductive and confuse young players.

During breaks

Keep it simple during breaks, such as halftime. Make sure all of your players are drinking water. Give them a few words of encouragement. If they've done something well as a team that follows something you've practiced, point that out. Don't try to offer lengthy commentary on the match so far or point out individual mistakes. End with a huddle and group team spirit shout-out.

After the game

After the final whistle, each team should line up and high five the opposing team on the field. Thank the officials for their part in the game today along with the opposing coach.

Win, lose, or draw, get the players together and give them some positive words. If it was a defeat, ask the players to point out some positive moments from the game. Keep the score in perspective for them and have them look forward to the next training session and game. And make sure the players don't forget any of their belongings as they are leaving!

Being the Woman or Man in the Middle

If you have multiple kids, you may already be used to playing "referee" among them to settle squabbles and disputes. If you're good at that, get ready — you may need those skills to referee on the soccer field as well!

REMEMBER

Unless you have a burning desire to actually be a referee and take the required courses, you'll likely only end up refereeing your kid's game at the recreational level for younger kids, where official referees are rarely provided. It's often the job of a coach or parent to keep order during the game.

TIP

Because the kids are so small and the stakes so low, don't stress out too much about this role. There are some benefits, though — having a go at refereeing will surely give you a greater appreciation for the challenges of the task, which develops a healthy respect for the role as your child progresses through the age groups.

Note: This section is about volunteer refereeing for kids under age 10, which is when you are most likely to be asked to help out as the person in the middle. If you are interested in refereeing at older and more competitive ages, you want to take official courses and certification. Your state youth soccer association can provide resources for this journey.

TIP

Your league or club may provide some basic refereeing instruction and materials, but this may not always be the case.

The following sections cover a few things you need to have and know to succeed as a volunteer referee.

Getting set for the kick

For a general overview of how soccer is played and the basic rules of the game, Chapter 1 gives you a primer. However, if you're refereeing, you need to know some specifics that vary by age group and league rules.

Some of the fundamental things to know and check on before the game kicks off are

>> **Ball size:** Refer to Table 1-2 in Chapter 1, which gives a guide to the right size ball for the right age group.

>> **Game length:** One of the main responsibilities of a referee is to keep time and stop play for any designated breaks, halftime, and the end of the game (full time). Make sure

you know how long each game is, when breaks are, and how long breaks should last.

>> **Number of players:** Each team cannot field more than the maximum number of players allowed per team. Be sure you know this number and enforce it throughout the game — count the players at the start of each half and check that when substitutions are made, the same number of players are coming off the field as are going on.

>> **Team uniforms:** Players on each team should be wearing their team uniforms, and the two uniforms should be distinct colors from each other so that you can distinguish what team each player is on.

Equipment

Referees in more senior matches need all sorts of equipment, but at the rec soccer level as a volunteer, you'll be glad to know you only need a couple of things: a whistle and a stopwatch.

The whistle is used to communicate the start and end of each period of play and to stop or restart play when needed.

One quick peep on the whistle signals it's time for the players to kick off, two peeps signal a break in play (such as halftime), and three peeps mark the full-time mark and the end of the game. When blowing the whistle to stop play, such as for a foul, give the whistle a good hearty peep so the players follow it.

A stopwatch is used to keep track of playing time. You need to know how long each period of play is and set a timer appropriately. You can use a watch you wear, a stopwatch you carry, or an app on your phone.

REMEMBER

At rec soccer youth level, you aren't expected to wear a proper referee uniform (in fact, you may look a bit silly if you dress up like a professional referee with a bunch of 5-year-olds running around!). Just wear whatever is comfortable to move around the field.

Making and explaining the right calls

The goal of refereeing kids under the age of 10 isn't to be a disciplinarian obsessing over the letter of the law and doling out punishments. The referee is there to keep the game organized, apply the basic structure of the game, and ensure that kids are learning the rules.

Importantly, this includes taking a moment to explain to them why something breaks the rules so they understand what they should do in the future. For example, if a player doesn't understand that the ball is out of play when it crosses the sideline, explain it to them rather than simply giving the ball to the other team and moving on.

REMEMBER

It's important to make sure you are following the right set of rules for the age group you are refereeing. The rules should be provided to you by your club or league.

Dealing with parents

One of the hardest parts of being a referee can be the comments from the sideline. At older and more competitive levels of soccer, verbal abuse of the referee is unfortunately common from over-zealous parents. I discuss the importance of respect for the referee in Chapter 6.

The good news for you as the referee at the preschool or elementary school ages is that parents usually have a much more relaxed and respectful attitude. They're generally just happy to see their kid out there, and winning or losing doesn't feel as if it matters as much.

That said, it's always good to set expectations and nip any loud commentary on refereeing decisions in the bud. You can have a quick word with parents before the game starts — remind them you, too, are a parent, you're volunteering to referee, and it's a recreational game of soccer. Some face-to-face moments can quickly remind everyone that it's all about making this fun for the kids.

TOPSOCCER

For players with disabilities, whether physical or emotional, most states have recreational programs designed to bring the opportunity to play and learn in the community. They're typically offered for players from the age of 5 to 21.

The official platform of US Youth Soccer that provides children with diverse abilities a safe and fun environment to play in is called TOPSoccer (which stands for **T**he **O**utreach **P**rogram for **S**occer).

TOPSoccer started back in the 1990s, and programs are now affiliated with state soccer associations across the nation. The cost to participate in TOPSoccer is usually kept very low to maximize its accessibility, and programs are often run by local youth soccer clubs. Sessions are usually offered weekly and typically last 45 minutes.

In the programs, players are grouped together to play soccer based on both ability and age. Each player is given a volunteer "buddy" to partner with one-to-one, providing mentoring support, encouragement, and joining in on fun activities.

To find the local TOPSoccer program near you, visit the US Youth Soccer website (www.usyouthsoccer.org).

2

Getting into Club Soccer

Figure out how to find and sign up for a club team.

Know what to do to be ready for a season of club play.

Help keep your kid healthy and find out how to deal with injuries that may occur.

Dive into some dedicated info if you have an aspiring goalkeeper.

Chapter **5**

Joining Competitive Club Soccer

S o far, so much fun — the recreational soccer programs covered in Part 1 focus on enjoyment and getting your kid outside kicking the ball around a couple of times a week. This chapter explores what it means to take the next step into joining a competitive club soccer program, where the focus shifts to more intense training and games with more focus on player development and results on the field.

Understanding Club Soccer

Most kids who end up playing on competitive club programs make that transition somewhere between the ages of 8 and 11. There's no definitive age that makes the most sense, though: While there may be some advantages to joining a club program earlier, making the switch too soon can backfire if your kid isn't ready. Consider carefully the benefits and challenges of moving from rec to competitive play.

Comparing competitive and recreational programs

When your child is around the age of 8, you'll be faced with a choice if they look to continue playing youth soccer. The organized youth soccer world diverges into two different organized environments, one known as "recreational" and one known as "competitive."

Recreational programs have lighter commitments. The level of participation expected and the intensity is lower, as compared to competitive programs, so there are fewer training sessions and less travel to games. The main focus is on teamwork and enjoyment.

Competitive programs are, as the name suggests, focused more on competition, including on winning games. There is a large emphasis on developing players' skills, and competitive teams demand more time commitment and travel for players (and parents!).

REMEMBER

The promise is that competitive programs should help your kid improve at soccer more rapidly than recreational play and put them on a pathway to potentially move up to more advanced levels of play.

TIP

In some states, "competitive" soccer is known as "travel" or "club" soccer. Whatever the interchangeable terminology, competitive club soccer is distinguished from "recreational" programs, which have lighter expectations for the volume and intensity of training and games and come at a lower cost.

Committing to competitive soccer

So, is your child ready for what is called "competitive" soccer? The number one consideration is to assess how committed your child is to the sport — and how committed you are to spend more time and money as they play at a more serious level.

Take the time to give serious consideration to the commitment required in playing competitive soccer. The seasons are longer, and training takes place multiple times per week. There will be games on weekends and an increasing amount of travel to matches and tournaments. There's also a significant cost increase. These elements are all outlined in detail later in this chapter.

TIP

Recreational soccer is a great option to continue to play, and a transition to competitive programs can always happen later. Don't feel pressured to sign up for competitive soccer just because it is seen as a "step up." Your child may have friends on their rec team and may not want to leave them; it's important to consider the social element of playing soccer as well as the competitive aspect. Many youth soccer clubs offer both recreational and competitive programs, so your child can always transition later.

Assessing ability

When making the decision on rec versus competitive soccer, you also need to consider your child's ability to compete at higher levels of play. Assessing their skill level and physical development can be hard, as of course we all see our children through rose-tinted lenses — your child may be a superstar on a rec team, but not quite so dominant at more competitive levels.

TIP

If your child struggles to perform strongly in recreational soccer, it may be that they aren't yet ready for competitive soccer. If they want to get there, further training and time for physical development may be all it takes. Your child can try out for a competitive program and make the leap later if it makes sense.

Maturity and desire

It's important to discuss the commitment and expectations of the program with your child and talk together about whether this is right for them, or whether they'd rather keep playing with a focus firmly on fun at the recreational level. Do they have the desire to improve, to work hard, and follow coaching instruction?

Competitive soccer brings with it more pressure and the emotional challenges of being benched or even cut from a team. Is your child ready and resilient enough for this?

What to expect in competitive soccer

There are no two ways around it — competitive soccer comes with a high expectation for the level of participation in team training, games, and tournaments.

The competitive soccer year generally runs for around ten months, though even in the summer, there's an expectation (if not an obligation) to continue development with camps or other off-season training programs.

If you feel your child would benefit from the competitive program, here's what you can expect to find:

>> **Professional coaches:** Recreational soccer programs often use a combination of volunteer parent coaches and professional coaches. In competitive soccer programs, you can expect all training and games to be led by a professional coach with the appropriate coaching qualifications for your child's level of play.

>> **Frequent training:** You can expect your child to go to training three times a week during each season, with sessions usually lasting 75 or 90 minutes. Training is highly structured with drills to improve individual skills and develop team tactics. Competitive teams usually train for ten months of the year.

TIP

Players are also encouraged, though not obliged, to practice soccer outside of the already extensive training obligations. Many players play at home for 30 to 60 minutes several times a week to work on their ball skills (see Chapter 9 for tips).

>> **Travel to games:** Your club team will likely play every weekend during the season against other teams in your area. Games are hosted by each club, which means traveling to

those locations. (This is why competitive soccer is also known as "travel" soccer.) Depending on the location of clubs, this can mean traveling an hour or more each weekend for a single match. This factor varies a lot by your geographic area and the density of local clubs to play against.

>> **Tournaments:** As well as regular games during the season, special tournaments take place during the year with teams from across your region. The number varies by club and area, but you can likely expect your child's team to play in two to four tournaments per year. These typically take place over a weekend with each team playing three or four games at each tournament.

REMEMBER

However good your child is from their natural talent, like in much of life, simply showing up is critical to success. Missing training frequently, not showing up to games without a good reason, or skipping tournaments will almost certainly mean that your child will not progress in the competitive soccer pathway.

If your child doesn't want to attend training or games, it's not likely to be helpful to force them to do so. This may make them resentful toward you and toward the sport, and it may mean they ultimately quit playing soccer altogether. Instead, talk through the challenges around the commitment with your child. If you can't resolve them, consider moving to a recreational program instead so they continue playing rather than quitting altogether.

Of course, there are many understandable reasons that a practice, game, or even tournament may need to be missed. These can vary from illness to other obligations or family travel. Whatever the reason, don't worry if there's a reasonable explanation to share with the team coach. It's also okay if your kid just needs a break from training once in a while.

REMEMBER

Competitive programs base a lot of their marketing on being the route to higher levels of play including college soccer or professional team academies. There is certainly some truth to this — competitive soccer programs provide highly structured player development environments and tournament play provides potential exposure to talent scouts. But it is not the exclusive way to reach higher levels of play, and there are certainly no guarantees that your child will win a college soccer scholarship, let alone become a professional player, just because they are on a competitive soccer program.

Picking a Program

If you and your child have now made the call to move to competitive soccer, you'll need to wade through various options. Those may be limited if you live in a small community with only one or two competitive soccer clubs. Or, in a large metropolitan area, there can be a dozen potential clubs to play for. There are a number of factors to consider as well as transitional options when making the leap.

Finding the right level of play

Because competitive soccer programs ultimately aim to funnel players by skill to the highest tiers of play, teams and competitions are divided by various levels of play based on each club's assessment of its players — including your child.

The reasons for separating teams by ability are logical: It creates closer competition in games and makes it easier for coaches to design drills and development plans for players with relatively similar levels of ability. It's no fun for a player to be on a team where they're by far the weakest player, or for a team of weaker players to get smashed every weekend by teams with much stronger players.

TIP

Unfortunately, there is no nationwide standardized vernacular for naming each level across clubs. Each club has its own name for various tiers, and some have more tiers than others — particularly larger youth soccer clubs in big metropolitan areas. Club websites usually provide an explanation of their different levels and the names they give them, but if you're unsure, reach out to the club through the contact information on the website and ask for more information.

Bridging rec to competitive soccer

If you've read through all the benefits and demands of your youngster heading into the world of competitive soccer, you may be glad to discover that many clubs offer programs that essentially serve as transitional bridges between recreational and competitive soccer. These programs are often aimed at kids between the ages of 8 and 11 who may be ready to move to more advanced soccer.

That means the commitment level and quality of training is a step above recreational, but without as much travel or selection competition as competitive travel programs.

TIP

Unlike most recreational programs, pre-competitive programs have fully licensed professional coaches instead of volunteers. The focus is less on fun and enjoyment and more on skill development and performing in games.

The vernacular for the names of these transitional programs varies, but they are often called "pre-competitive." The programs cost more than recreational soccer but less than fully competitive travel programs.

Assessing club teams

Many recreational soccer teams are run by organizations that also have competitive soccer arms. If that's the case for your child's existing rec program, that can make for the easiest transition.

If you don't have that option and need to join a club entirely new to you, a good starting point is your state youth soccer association's official website. You can usually find a directory there or even a map with locations of all officially affiliated clubs.

Your local state will only list clubs that are officially affiliated with the association. This means they are compliant with state association standards covering areas such as player insurance and competing in official competitions.

Word of mouth is often the best way to find a club. Ask other parents who may have kids playing club soccer to see if they have any advice or insight. Your rec team coach may also have suggestions, as they are likely connected into the local youth soccer community.

To try to understand the reputation of a club, it's important to get more than one opinion. A single one-off opinion may not be representative of the experience as a whole.

When examining different clubs, see if you can find out some key information from their websites or by contacting clubs. Following are some questions to consider.

Where does the club practice and play games?

With multiple practices and games a week, life will be an awful lot easier if the club's facilities are convenient to your home. Check club websites for listings of their facility locations.

Clubs may practice and play matches at multiple facilities. If you're not sure where a club plays, reach out to the contact information for them listed on the website.

How many teams does the club have per age group?

Larger clubs may sound great in theory — obviously they are doing something right if they are retaining a large number of players — and they may have more options with more teams playing at different levels.

Larger clubs will likely offer a less personal touch because they are managing so many different teams and players. Smaller clubs can have a closer community feel and be more attentive to families. The decision between a larger or smaller club may come down to the kind of culture and experience your family is looking for.

What are the levels of play in each age group?

Most clubs have multiple levels dividing teams by ability. Take a look at how many different levels are offered and how many teams are at each level. It's easier for your child to be placed at a level appropriate for their ability if the club has plenty of options on offer from players transitioning from rec soccer up to elite levels of play.

What competitions does the club participate in?

This question will get you into exploring the complex world of youth soccer structures, which are difficult to follow, but nevertheless it's helpful to know which competitions the club participates in.

If the club is affiliated with the official state soccer association, they'll be part of various sanctioned leagues and tournaments that fall under the state association's umbrella. Club websites usually explain which competitions their teams participate in and the levels of play they fall into.

TIP

When you are first joining a competitive program, especially between the ages of 8 and 12, don't worry too much about whether the club has teams in the highest regional or national elite competitions. If your kid is or becomes good enough for higher levels of play, there's always the option to move clubs if needed. The priority initially should be finding a good club that fits other important criteria to get playing successfully.

How far do teams travel to play?

When you're just starting out in club soccer, it can be a shock to see how far teams often travel for games and tournaments.

Much of this will be determined by the geography of your area and the density of soccer clubs. Coastal areas abundant with clubs like California or New York may require less travel than more sparsely populated areas in the mountains or plains in the middle of America (though places like Texas or Chicago are exceptions here!).

Some clubs work to minimize travel as much as possible to keep costs down. The fact that a club travels farther for its games isn't necessarily a sign that the level of play is somehow better.

Within clubs, teams at different levels of play may travel less or more. Advanced-level teams often travel farther to play other advanced teams in regional or national competitions and tournaments. Make sure you understand what the travel landscape looks like for each level of play.

What experience do the coaches have?

The quality of any youth soccer experience comes down to a large degree on the coaching. These are the women and men who will be spending the most time on the soccer field with your child, several hours a week.

It's not possible to know everything about a coach until you've seen them out there on the field interacting with their teams and your child, but you can look up or ask about their experience. A solid record of playing soccer at the collegiate level or professionally is usually a bare minimum, but not all good players become good coaches, so look to see whether they have a track record of coaching youth soccer.

What's the club's history?

The only constant in the youth soccer world seems to be change, and that includes clubs, with new ones forming and old ones fading away or changing names as they're taken over by larger clubs.

Most clubs will outline their history on the "about" page of their website. Some clubs may date back as far as the 1970s, while others may be much fresher. Like many things, plenty of longevity for an organization is a good sign of consistently solid service to the community.

If a club is newer, it's a good idea to ask about what has driven its emergence. Is it serving a new expanding part of town, a different constituency of players, a breakaway from another club, or a newly established entity affiliated with a professional team?

Longevity doesn't guarantee quality — leadership changes or other factors can rapidly shift the dynamic of any organization. Word of mouth in the community can be helpful to understand the club's current reputation.

What's the club's record of producing elite-level players?

The top clubs tend to produce plenty of elite players who go on to play in college or professionally. They often list these accomplishments proudly on their websites to show their strength in elite player development. If this is a path your child wants to go on, it's a good sign if the club has a strong track record.

Make sure those accomplishments are relevant to your child's gender: Some clubs have much stronger boys programs than girls and vice versa.

Only a small number of players go on to play high-level college or professionally. Particularly when starting out in competitive soccer, following that pathway just because a club has a strong track record isn't any guarantee of getting there, nor is it the only way to get there. Your child may move clubs later to play more elite soccer, or they may end up just enjoying playing with no ambition to play at the highest levels.

How much are the club fees?

You'll certainly want to compare the base fees each club charges as they can vary quite widely. See "Paying to Play" later in this chapter for more on fees and costs of playing club soccer.

If you can, attend a practice or event held by the club you are considering. This can give you some insight into the culture of the club.

Going to tryouts

Players are usually assessed by clubs and placed at a certain level of play via an open tryout that any player can register for and attend. Tryouts provide the opportunities for coaches to evaluate the abilities, skill level, and potential of your child and the others attending. The session may include drills and scrimmages giving players the chance to show their technical quality, physical level, and tactical understanding of soccer. Coaches assess players to determine which (if any) of their club's teams they may be a fit to join.

REMEMBER

Tryouts are usually held right at the end of each soccer year — typically in May or June. This leads into teams making their decisions on roster placements ahead of the next season.

Getting set for trying out

Prepare for tryouts with regular practice in the weeks leading up to it, including getting some extra touches outside of regular team practice. Feeling confident with the ball and being sharp at tryouts is important to attract the coach's attention.

Tryouts can be daunting for both kids and parents. It can feel as if your kid's every kick might determine their soccer future, and they only have an hour or two to catch the eye of watching coaches grading every player.

REMEMBER

It's important to understand that tryouts are not the be-all and end-all for player placement. Clubs and their coaches assess players throughout the year, and it's not uncommon for changes to be made even during the season if a player is at a level that's obviously too low or too high for their ability.

At the end of the year, along with performance at tryouts, the club's assessment of a player's level takes into account observations made throughout the season in determining the placements for the following year.

Registering for tryouts

You can't just show up to club tryouts unannounced, even if they are promoted as "open." Make sure you register in advance — there'll usually be a deadline to sign up a week or so before the tryout date(s). Most of the time, there won't be a fee for club tryouts, but this may vary depending on the program.

TIP

If you're on an existing team, tryouts are a good way to explore potentially moving to another club. You may want to do this for various reasons, including to see whether your child would be placed at a different level or whether you want to leave your current club and find a new place to play. Tryout season is typically the time to do this, prior to registering for the next year's play.

Attending tryouts

Make sure you arrive early at the tryout, at least 20 minutes before the scheduled arrival time. If you haven't played at this club before, you may be unfamiliar with the parking situation and the field location, so it's good to build in some buffer time. It'll also give your child some extra time to warm up and get comfortable.

Once you're there, you'll need to check in at a registration table. Your child will probably be given a bib with an identifying number on it to wear so the coaches can tell who is who and make notes as the tryout progresses.

If you can, try to briefly introduce yourself and your child to the coaching staff. Don't try to overwhelm them with conversation and questions, especially before the tryout, as they'll have a lot going on. But it's a good idea to put names to faces for them.

REMEMBER

Once the tryout starts, it's time to stay on the sideline and out of the way. The tryout will consist of some warm-ups and then a series of drills and scrimmages to assess the kids in playing conditions.

What do coaches look for at the tryouts? Typically, they assess

>> **Technical ability:** Coaches look at players' fundamental soccer skills: the ability to control the ball efficiently, plus passing, shooting, and defensive qualities. These are important to coaches as they are at the core of potential high performance.

>> **Physical qualities:** Speed, strength, and stamina are critical physical elements that are looked at. Children grow and develop at different rates, so coaches should try not to over-index on physical strength; it's possible that within a few months, many of the kids at any given tryout will look very different.

>> **Game understanding:** The mental side of the game — knowing how to move to the right positions on the soccer field to attack and defend — is often the deciding factor that separates levels among players with similar technical and physical attributes. Players who see the game well and can make good soccer decisions are more likely to be placed on higher-level teams.

>> **Teamwork and communication:** As important as individual skills are, soccer is a team sport — coaches look for players who can contribute to the whole team's success. That means players who know when to be unselfish — to pass the ball or run hard to cover defensive positions — are assessed well. Good communicators on the field who can provide leadership and set a good example are also valued highly.

TIP

Although it's your kid trying out to play at a club, if this is your first look at how a club operates, treat it as a chance to "try out" the club yourself. Keep an eye on how well the tryout is organized. Are the communication and organization good? Are the field conditions satisfactory? Are the coaches attentive and positive in their interactions with the players? This is a great opportunity to get to know the club and see whether there are any red flags that should have you consider alternatives.

What to expect after tryouts

Immediately after the tryout, it's best to provide some positive reinforcement to your child, but it's not the moment to analyze what has just happened. Emotions can often run high after tryouts, so it's better to let your child rest physically and mentally. Let your young player know that however they performed, many factors go into club placements and there'll be plenty of opportunity in the future regardless of where it lands this time.

The club should communicate to you when team placements will be shared to families following the tryout, but it's often pretty fast — within a few days.

REMEMBER

The level at which your child is placed isn't dependent only on how they performed. Many other factors you have no access to understand also determine which child is placed on which team. Each team has a given number of roster spots, and many will already be taken up by existing players. Some players may move up or down between teams at different levels. Sometimes, entire teams are added or removed by clubs depending on the demand they have or coaches that are available. Fortune and circumstance play a role in which spots can be offered.

Once the coaches have finished placing players, you'll receive an email with the news of the team your child has been offered a place on. The message will give you a deadline to accept or reject the placement, which is often done via an online registration.

TIP

Make sure that you understand the fees that will be due (if any) for the club and team you are joining. More advanced teams have higher fees than lower-level teams, and some clubs are more expensive in general than others. See the next section for a full understanding of what to expect.

Paying to Play

You may want to sit down for this one: Competitive youth soccer can end up costing an arm, a leg, and even a couple more body parts! Well, not quite, but it's an expensive endeavor, receiving criticism from parents who wonder whether it's all worth it as well as from critics who say the cost prevents a lot of good players from taking part.

REMEMBER

There's no doubt the monetary cost is high: The sticker shock of registration fees that cost into the thousands is only the start, as additional expenses in the form of uniforms, tournament fees, and travel expenditure layer on further. The justification is that it costs a lot to operate a club and for professional service to take place and bills to be paid, and these costs need to be borne by parents.

Registration costs

The main and most visible cost you will pay is the registration fee for each year. These costs vary widely between clubs. Larger clubs, particularly those affiliated with professional teams or that have a reputation for developing large numbers of elite players, typically charge higher fees. Clubs justify this by saying the higher fees are needed to cover the expenses of higher-end facilities, top coaches, and other administrative support.

Even within a club, these fees often vary depending on the age of the player and the level they are playing at. That's because the more advanced and competitive the level, the more training sessions and time the player will spend with the club and the more the club will spend on the costs of serving higher-level players.

The range for competitive clubs can be anywhere from $1,500 to over $3,000 per year for each player to participate. Some clubs offer the option to pay these fees in installments instead of just in one lump sum, which can help spread out the financial burden.

REMEMBER

Even if you stay at the same club year over year, you'll need to register every year and pay to sign up for the coming season. This confirms to the club that your child will be a "returning player" so they can get an accurate count on numbers and start receiving your cash! If you don't register — and don't worry, the club will certainly send you reminders to do so — the club will assume your child isn't returning, and at a certain point your child will lose the spot they have on their current team.

TIP

Many clubs do offer financial support in the form of scholarships for kids from families who meet certain criteria. This may be dependent on factors such as your geographic location and household income falling under a certain threshold. It's worth asking the club if such support is available if otherwise you may not be able to afford the fees to participate.

Purchasing uniforms

Uniform costs are not usually included in the fees for competitive programs and come at a substantial additional expense. Uniforms consist of a jersey, shorts, and socks. You'll need to purchase a set of these in both "home" and "away" colors. In addition, you'll likely be asked or even required to purchase an additional "training" kit to wear to practice — also a jersey, shorts, and socks. If that's not enough, you may also be expected to purchase a team backpack as well.

TIP

On top of that set of gear, you'll likely be offered a myriad of other items to purchase that come branded with club colors and logo. That can include training items for cold weather such as a jacket, hoodie, or long pants. Although it can be nice to buy branded gear, remember these items aren't usually required and you can likely purchase unbranded options for lower prices online or at sporting goods stores.

The total cost for a uniform purchase can easily total $300–$400. Your club will provide information on how to order; this is usually done through a third-party uniform provider. You will need to follow the instructions on how to order online. Make sure you follow the sizing guide on the website to get the right size for your child.

TIP

Order a kit very slightly too large for your child, and certainly don't order something likely to be snug-fitting at first. Your kid will be wearing the uniform for at least one year, and potentially two, so you'll want to make sure they don't grow out of it too fast.

Most clubs have the same uniforms on a two-year cycle. This means you'll need to purchase a new set of uniforms after every two seasons, regardless of whether your child still fits into the previous set. If you're unlucky, and your child happens to join a club when it's on the second year of a two-year cycle, you may need to buy a new uniform two years in a row.

REMEMBER

If your child is a goalkeeper, they'll be ordering a different set of goalkeeper-specific uniforms. These will come in different colors from the outfield players.

Covering tournament fees

You may think that your registration fee covers the cost of all the games your child plays each season, but unfortunately, you may well need to dig into your pockets again. At many clubs, fees for weekend-long tournaments featuring teams from various clubs are actually an additional charge.

This payment is often separate from regular team fees because the tournament organizers have to rent out a large number of additional fields, hire referees and medical providers, and pay for administrators — costs that are then passed back to clubs and ultimately to you.

TIP

These fees can vary widely across different regions, but expect to pay $50–$100 for a weekend tournament held locally and more for an out-of-state tournament when you may also be covering costs for your coach's travel and other expenses.

Assessing travel expenses

A less direct but nonetheless still very real expense is the cost of travel. It's hard to assess how much this will cost, since it depends largely on how far are you traveling — and by what means — to soccer training, regular weekend games, and tournaments.

Unless you happen to live right next to a soccer facility hosting all of that for your team, the cost of gas — given that most larger competitive soccer facilities do require a car to get to — will start to add up.

REMEMBER

Where it can really get expensive, though, is out-of-state travel that occurs at elite levels of play for kids typically 12 years and older. A couple of out-of-state tournaments per year is not unusual for players on advanced teams, and the cost of flights, hotels, and food for you and your child can easily hit $1,000 per trip. See Chapter 13 for more on elite programming.

Chapter **6**

Getting into the Club Soccer Season

et ready: Your weekends, many evenings, plenty of dollars, and a lot of mental, emotional, and physical effort will be expended by you and your soccer player in the first season of competitive club soccer play and beyond! This chapter explores the people you'll need to know at your club, what you need to get ready for games and tournaments, how you can help your club out as a volunteer parent — and even how to start planning for season two and beyond.

Getting to Know Your Club

Whether large or small, your competitive soccer club is comprised of the people who run it and the facilities you play at, both of which you will need to quickly familiarize yourself with. Connecting with the coaches and administrators and building good relationships can help smooth out any challenges, and you can engage even further into the club soccer experience if you can find the free time to volunteer.

Interacting with the coach

It's fair to say that a coach can make or break your child's soccer experience. Much like teachers at school, an exceptional coach who really connects with their kids and drives them forward can mean the world. On the flip side, a coach without good skills with kids and who can't organize their group of players effectively is unlikely to build a good bond with the team or your child and can impede their development.

REMEMBER

While most things about youth soccer clubs can be researched prior to signing up, every club has a mix of coaches and there's a bit of blind luck to who your kid ends up with. You may hear feedback about a certain coach through the grapevine, but it's best to keep an open mind until you see them working with the team.

TIP

Sometimes it can take a few weeks or even longer for the positive impact of a coach to really be felt by a team. Don't make a hasty judgment a week into the season unless there are very large red flags that need to be raised to the club hierarchy. Wait and see how the team bonds and builds over a period of many weeks.

There will often be an opportunity before the season starts to meet the coach if the club holds an orientation event, as many do. This is a good chance to introduce yourself and your child and get to know the coach a little better prior to the first game of the season.

REMEMBER

Most coaches in youth soccer aren't coaching full time, even at competitive levels. They are often juggling the challenging schedules of youth soccer practices, games, and tournaments with other responsibilities to pay the bills. Many may coach more than one team as well as holding down other work. They are likely coaching because they are passionate about soccer and want to inspire young players.

Communicating with coaches

When and how should you communicate with your child's coach? This is an area that can often trip up parents, creating difficult situations for coaches or staff, often around issues that may not actually be a problem for their child. Emotions can often run high after games and result in parents hastily sending messages that exacerbate challenges. Sending frequent messages questioning every other decision by a coach isn't likely to be productive for anyone.

TIP

It's a good idea to wait at least 24 — if not 48 — hours before sending a message to a coach on an issue you have a concern about. This allows time for emotions to settle down.

REMEMBER

Your starting assumption should be that your coach is doing their best for all the players on their team — including your child. They are qualified, probably experienced, and spending plenty of time every week trying to balance a number of factors you have little insight into. Starting from a position of grace, understanding, and respect for coaches sets a good example for your child and helps mitigate hasty assumptions.

All of that said, it's absolutely a good idea to have a positive relationship with the coach, ask relevant questions about their approach to coaching, and get their input on your child's development. Coaches are generally happy that parents are interested and care about all the work they are putting in with the team.

TIP

Make sure to attend any preseason meetings the coach or club holds. This is often where expectations are laid out regarding how communication with the coach should be structured.

Key club contacts to know

Club soccer teams are typically structured in a way that means you'll hear from and communicate with two other main points of contact aside from the team coaches: the director of coaching and the club administrator.

Director of coaching

Most clubs will have a *director of coaching*, or DOC for short, who is responsible for the overall development of a set of teams within the club. There will usually be a different DOC for the girls' and boys' programs, and they will span a certain age range to oversee.

Ultimately, the DOC is the boss of your team's coach (and other coaches at the club). It's the DOC's job to hire, train, and develop coaches within the club's system, oversee roster construction (which players go on which teams), and ensure that player development is positive. You won't have a lot of direct contact with the director of coaching, though you'll likely hear from them via email or in preseason meetings and occasional other communications.

REMEMBER

DOCs will periodically attend team training sessions and games to understand how coaches are operating and will be present at all team tournaments, but don't expect to see them every week. They are responsible for multiple teams, and the coach is their link to those teams and parents.

Ideally, you will rarely need to reach out to or communicate directly with the DOC. Issues around playing on the field should be handled by the team coach, and off-the-field operational challenges with the team administrator (see the next section). However, if you have a major concern with the coach or a question about the direction of the club as a whole, this can be raised with the DOC directly.

TIP

It's a good idea to get to know the DOC if there's an opportunity to interact with them at an event. If there is an issue you need to address, having some prior personal contact with them can be helpful.

Administrator

The nuts and bolts of a youth soccer club working well for everyone depend on a highly undervalued role — the club *administrator*. The administrator is responsible for ensuring that the club is functioning operationally; communicating well; and supporting coaches, directors, volunteers, and staff. That includes managing the player registration process and rosters, supporting event and travel planning, and coordinating fields and facilities.

REMEMBER

The administrator, not your player's coach, is your first port of call if you have questions or issues with the registration process or other operational issues or challenges.

Team manager

The club administrator is responsible for multiple teams at once. The organizer of many of the logistical pieces and group activities is a dedicated *team manager*, who helps with everything from communicating schedules to making sure the kids have snacks for halftime.

REMEMBER

The team manager is almost always a volunteer parent. Like you, they have a lot going on and they've raised their hand to help out, so be patient as they work through helping to organize the team.

Familiarizing yourself with the facilities

Your club likely has a permanent home base or, depending on the size of the club, multiple facilities that serve different regions. For example, a club may have west and east regions that draw players from those areas of your town or city. They may each have their own primary practice facility and hold games in a convenient location for that area so that players (and parents!) don't need to travel further to practice and play.

The size of the facility and number of fields depends on the club's size and whether it is sharing with other clubs or has an exclusive lease or ownership of the facility. During the winter, depending on the climate of your region, clubs may also run practices and camps at indoor facilities, usually on artificial turf.

REMEMBER

Either way, before the first practices and games, be sure you're familiar with the facility locations and parking instructions for where you need to go, which should all be laid out on your club's website.

Volunteering for the team

I cover volunteer coaching and refereeing at the recreational level in Chapter 4, but you can contribute in other ways to make the team soccer experience as fun as it can be for everyone involved by helping out at the competitive club level.

The most common volunteer position in competitive club soccer is that of the team manager (see the earlier section "Team manager"). Now, don't worry, this doesn't mean that you're managing the team on the field at practices or games — leave that to the coach! It means you're helping to manage the team's activities by liaising with the coach and the club.

There are lots of benefits to being involved with your child's team as a team manager. You can help foster a positive environment for your kid and their teammates, supporting the growth of camaraderie and assisting with good organization of activities and clear communication between the parents and coach.

So what will you be asked to do as a team manager? Typically, duties include the following:

>> Help communicate training and game schedules and inform parents of any important changes or updates.

>> Organize social events for the team to increase bonding among coaches, parents, and players.

>> If needed, support organization of travel for the team.

>> Assist with team registration and check-in for tournaments.

>> Arrange a snack schedule for parents to rotate bringing refreshments to each game.

>> Collect funds for an end-of-season gift to give to the coach.

Perhaps the most important role of all is to be at the heart of generating a strong sense of togetherness around the team. Doing the duties that I mention earlier, efficiently helps, along with being a positive influence on the sidelines and helping everyone stay focused on the kids enjoying their time on the field and becoming friends off it.

TIP

Volunteering is a great way to get to know the club better. You'll spend more time with club staff helping to organize the team and get an inside track on how everything works, which can be helpful as a parent.

REMEMBER

Volunteering is a time-consuming responsibility on top of a lot of time you'll likely already spend playing chauffeur to practices and games and supporting your child's activities. Be sure that you can comfortably commit to the time required for the tasks required, which may take up a few hours each week of the season.

TIP

Don't be afraid to ask other parents to help out, as this not only can provide you with backup and support but also help further integrate the group as a supportive unit for the team.

Here are some things you are *not* expected to do as a team manager — it's important that your role is clear and that you're not involved in the coaching of the team on the field:

>> You are not getting involved in discussions about playing time for any individuals — parents with concerns about this should communicate directly with the coach.

>> You aren't going to be on the sideline or engaged in coaching the team, unless you have another specific role as an assistant coach.

Kicking Off the Right Way

They say 90 percent of success in life is just showing up. In youth soccer, that may also be true, but to be ready to show up for the season takes quite a bit of planning. You need to understand when and where you have to get your child, what to do to get your kid in the right uniform, and how to be prepared for the vagaries of the weather.

Kitting out

Club teams at the competitive levels are strict on players all wearing the same uniform, with matching jerseys, shorts, and socks.

REMEMBER

Most clubs change their uniforms every couple of years, in part driven by agreements with the uniform manufacturer. This means you may need to buy a new set even before your kid has outgrown their current uniforms.

Compared to getting uniforms for rec teams, at competitive clubs the process can be a slightly more complicated one that involves purchasing the uniform from a third-party vendor online.

You'll receive instructions from the league or club you have joined on how to do this; it often includes being sent a website link to follow and order from. You'll need to select the right size for your child and pay a separate fee to complete the purchase.

TIP

Make sure you order the right size uniform for your kid. You don't want to order items that are even slightly small on your child — this can be uncomfortable for athletic play and your youngster will quickly grow out of it. That said, don't order anything too oversized or your kid will be swimming in their uniform. Follow the sizing guide on the ordering page to get it right!

Following game and practice schedules

Keeping track of where and when your child needs to be somewhere for an activity can often feel like a part-time job in itself as a parent. Youth soccer certainly adds to this with its array of practices, camps, matches, and tournaments to add to already busy calendars.

You need to keep close track of all of these events and their locations and times — along with any subsequent updates or changes — because it's certainly not fun to realize you've shown up at the wrong time or location for a match.

Clubs usually share training, match, and tournament dates a couple of weeks prior to the season starting. Training schedules usually come first, as they start prior to matches, and they should have all of the time and location details you'll need to plan for.

Double-check the location of each practice before you set out. Sometimes a different facility or field may be used versus the regular location.

Exact match timings, opponents, and field locations may not be shared until after training for the season begins, as it can often take some time for administrators and coaches to finalize details across multiple clubs. Once the details for matches are buttoned up, they'll be added to your team's shared calendar.

Match schedules are subject to change as seasons go on due to various reasons — from facility scheduling challenges to team and player availability. Be sure to open all emails and read all texts from the club to stay up-to-date on any adjustments.

Tournament weekends will be known prior to the season starting, but the exact dates and details of matchups and game times will likely not be finalized until a couple of weeks prior to them taking place.

Even if tournament details aren't known in full detail, take note of the weekend dates, and if you intend for your child to take part, keep that weekend clear of other events.

Taking on tournaments

Tournament play presents an opportunity for a whole weekend of games and even the chance to come away with a trophy. These special events are in addition to the regular slate of games scheduled for your team and see numerous clubs take part.

Your team will typically play three or four matches in a tournament, usually starting on a Friday and ending on a Sunday, though sometimes days will differ. Teams are organized into brackets by age group and level of play.

There is often a group stage of play with the top teams advancing to a final championship match. Winners and runners-up will usually receive trophies or medals, held at a presentation ceremony at the end of the tournament — a great photo moment if your kid's team makes it there!

Your team may choose to participate in two or three tournaments per season. Tournaments are usually repeating annual events organized to feature teams from multiple clubs across a certain region. You'll most likely first encounter locally arranged tournaments featuring teams from within one regional area, which may require you to travel depending on the location.

Youth soccer tournaments are major events and massive logistical feats of organization by the hosting club or association. Depending on the size of the area's youth soccer club community, a tournament can feature dozens of clubs, hundreds of teams, thousands of players, and tens of thousands of spectating parents and family members. The tournament may take place in multiple facilities in one area in order to secure enough fields to play on.

Tournaments are essentially soccer jamborees — you'll likely find food and drink vendors and even other activities organized around the fields.

When it comes to tournament time, you'll essentially need to clear your weekend schedule. As well as the confirmed games, additional playoff or championship games may be added on the last day depending on how your child's team performs.

Be prepared with plenty of sunscreen, snacks, and water, primarily for your child, but also for yourself and anyone else in your family attending.

At older ages or in elite youth play, regional and even national tournaments are organized that require interstate travel. See Chapter 13 for more on tournaments at this level.

Benefiting from carpooling

Getting your kid to team practice three times a week — perhaps even more often if they have additional specialized training — can be quite a grind. That's when the magic of the carpool can come to the rescue if you are fortunate to live close enough to other families on the team so that you can coordinate rides together.

The first thing to do is to figure out who lives where among the families on the team. This can be done through in-person conversations at the first couple of practices as you get to know the other parents, or if you have a team communication channel set up among the parents, you can send a message to see if anyone is in your area.

Once you've established that one or more families are nearby, it's just a matter of determining which days you'll rotate the duty of picking up the kids and driving them to and from practice. Of course, the rotation of making the drives is expected to be roughly fair and even, though if something comes up for a parent or guardian and that needs to be switched around, everyone should understand.

TIP

Be sure to communicate in advance if an issue arises and your child won't be going to practice so that the carpool plan can be adjusted. You don't want to leave it to the last minute if you can help it and force other parents to make last-minute adjustments to their schedule.

REMEMBER

As well as carpooling for training, if you're in a pinch and can't take your child to an actual game, reach out to other parents and see if someone else can help out. You'll almost certainly find a family who can assist and ensure that your child doesn't miss a game.

Knowing when weather stops play

Soccer can be played in a variety of weather conditions, from sun to rain and even (to some degree) snow. It's similar in this respect to the more traditionally known version of football in the United States.

That said, weather conditions can lead to games, practices, or tournaments being paused or cancelled. The two main reasons this can happen are to ensure player safety and to resolve any issues of playability on the field.

Player safety

Lightning in the area is the most common weather-related reason for a practice or game to be stopped. Coaches and administrators are instructed to stop play if lightning can present any risk to players. Many clubs instruct coaches to prevent play if there is a lightning strike within a 10-mile radius of the field. The area must remain clear of lightning for a certain period of time, often at least 30 minutes, before play can resume.

TIP

Some soccer facilities have automatic lightning alert systems that sound warnings when lightning is detected nearby. Other times, coaches are informed via an app or message from the club administrator that they must pause play.

Other dangerous weather conditions can also enforce a stoppage in play, such as hail or the threat of tornadoes, blizzards, or very strong winds.

Soccer can usually be played in cold or wet weather, though players are at risk of more injury at very cold temperatures, and it can be very uncomfortable or dangerous to be outside for long at extremely cold temperatures. Play is also stopped in those cases. Hot weather doesn't usually stop play, but extreme heat may do so for player safety reasons. At a minimum, additional water breaks may be added. Essentially, any weather condition that threatens player safety means coaches should stop play and ensure that youth players are not at risk.

TIP

Keep an eye on the weather forecast before games, especially if bad conditions are likely. While they may not stop play, you will want to be prepared on the sideline with an umbrella, rain jacket, or blanket depending on the conditions!

Field conditions

Weather conditions can also render the field unplayable for soccer. This happens more often on real grass pitches versus artificial turf. Heavy precipitation can make a grass pitch become too saturated with water — you can't kick a ball through a massive puddle.

Groundskeepers are concerned about real grass pitches being destroyed if games are played when the fields are soaked. Snow can also make a field unplayable. These decisions are usually made by the facility manager, ideally in advance of games to prevent you from traveling to a game that ultimately cannot take place.

REMEMBER

Many clubs list current field status on their websites, though more urgent alerts will likely be sent to you via text message or app alerts, so make sure you're paying attention to your phone on game days.

Behaving on the Sidelines

Watching your child play can be an emotional experience as a parent. You may have seen in the news concerns about parental behavior at youth sporting events — and rightly so, when it's aggressive to referees, negative to players, or obnoxious in general. But it's helpful to take a step back and understand that the root of the challenge comes from the amount of emotion most parents experience when watching their child participate in a competitive event.

As a parent, it's important to contain those emotions and remember the experience of the children on the field is what really matters. Arguing with the referee, telling your child to do something in the game that may clash with a coach's instruction, or screaming from the sidelines may create a negative experience for your child or other children as well as for the referee and coaches. So what should we do — and not do — as parents spectating at games?

Remembering that winning isn't everything

The objective of any game is, of course, to win it. The kids playing will be keeping track of the score and will want to win — there's nothing wrong with that. However, that's not all that *matters* about youth sports. These are, after all, children playing and not professional athletes whose salaries depend on results.

The important thing is to keep the score in perspective and not to let yourself, as the parent, get into the mindset that winning or losing is everything. There is a larger journey of developing as a player and a human that's part of the experience of youth sports to focus on.

TIP

While the goal is to win each game a team starts, in competitive youth soccer the coach will also be setting other goals for their team to achieve during the season. These may be about adapting to new tactics, focusing on passing, or defending strongly, and can vary throughout the season. Often short-term results are subservient to bigger plans to develop individual and team skills over the course of the season. Focusing only on winning individual games can be short-sighted, and pressure from parents to win can get in the way of heading toward longer-term achievements.

REMEMBER

In particular, don't get so wrapped up in the score that you think you need to somehow interject to influence the result — by berating the referee or trying to coach your kid from the sideline. Not only is this likely to be counterproductive, it's a poor example to set for your child.

Playing youth sports is ultimately about development as an athlete and as a teammate. Winning and losing are part of that, but there's much more to be taken from participating in the sport aside from focusing just on winning.

Cheering your team the right way

In some successful and prominent soccer-playing countries, such as Germany, parents often have to follow one simple rule on the sideline — be quiet! This clear directive prevents a challenge that seems to plague youth soccer in sports, a spiral of yelling that in extreme — but unfortunately not particularly rare — cases leads to parents confronting referees.

Many leagues in the United States have now tried enforcing silence on the sidelines, though more often, they encourage parents to focus on positive reinforcement. In fact, many youth soccer clubs now ask parents to follow a code of conduct, including agreements on this that you need to sign among the many pieces of digital paperwork that are part of your child's registration.

This is essentially a pledge that typically includes reasonable expectations on what to do and what not to do when attending games.

You will likely be asked to

>> Be respectful to referees, players, coaches, and fellow parents/spectators of the opposing team.

>> Applaud good efforts, play, and positive sporting behavior by players on both teams.

>> Be supportive of your team's coaches,

>> Follow any request from game officials.

You will likely be asked *not* to

>> Use bad or abusive language or obscene gestures in any circumstance at any game or practice

>> Make any verbal comments or gestures toward the match officials

>> Come within two yards of the sideline

>> Consume any alcohol at a practice or game

Respecting the referee

There's a reason youth sports have a crisis in securing enough people to referee games, and unfortunately, the primary reason is due to parental behavior on the sidelines. This can range from verbal abuse — yelling, insults, or threats — to aggressive gestures and even, though rarely, physical attacks.

REMEMBER

Referees in youth sports are very often teenagers learning the ropes in the role, just as impressionable as the players on the field. They are doing their best and deserve respect and understanding as part of the ecosystem of youth sports that develops future players and officials to be part of the sport.

If you haven't been to a youth sports event, talk of confrontational behavior by parents may shock you. After all, the stakes hardly seem high enough for such aggressive attitudes and behavior to develop. Unfortunately, the level of emotion around our children, the focus on winning being the be-all and end-all, and a serious disrespect for match officials as human beings have become all too common in many youth sports, including soccer.

In fact, it's so common that a majority of youth sports officials now report having experienced abuse. Given that the role does not pay lucratively and many referees are young and inexperienced, it's no wonder this fact has led to an increasing rate of attrition in retaining referees and has made it harder for youth sport organizations to recruit new ones. As well as parental abuse, referees are often also on the receiving end of poor behavior from players and coaches.

REMEMBER

The consequences of abusing a referee can be significant for the individual, causing anxiety and stress that lasts far beyond game day, especially for younger referees. Imagine trying to do your job and having an irate person yelling at you or threatening you.

TIP

As a parent on the sideline, you can help set an example by never making comments or any gestures toward a match official. If another parent does so, politely remind them the referee deserves respect and may be learning on the job themselves.

Assessing the Current Season

As your first season in club soccer comes to a close, it's time to both review how the year has gone and look ahead to the next one. Clubs start reviewing staff performance, evaluating their players, and planning their rosters as one season ends in order to be ready for the next one. Parents need to do the same.

Feedback is an important two-way street for the club and your player. The club needs to know from you how your child's experience was, along with every other player, to understand where there may be consistent issues to address. These may relate to coaching, facilities, or communication from the club.

You'll likely receive an end-of-season survey with a series of questions about your player's experience, which is often anonymous so you can be as honest as possible.

REMEMBER

If you have serious concerns about your coach or any other issue with the club, especially relating to player safety, don't wait until the end of the season or for a feedback survey to submit it. Flag anything significant to club administration as early as possible so that it can be addressed. See the section "Staying Safe Around the Soccer Field," later in this chapter, for more on this.

Most teams have their coaches perform player evaluations at the end of the year and sometimes at additional intervals during the season.

This feedback may include reviewing technical aspects of play, how the player contributes as a teammate, and areas for improvement to focus on moving forward.

The coach's evaluation often arrives in written form, though some coaches prefer to deliver the feedback directly to players and their parents (depending on the child's age).

Some clubs are now making the evaluations a collaborative experience, asking players to also give their thoughts on what they have enjoyed and goals they want to work on.

REMEMBER

The formal evaluations can provide helpful feedback for your player but don't place too much emphasis on it for your child. They can be formulaic at times, and not all coaches are as good at paperwork as they are coaching on the field.

TIP

Don't wait until the end of the season to get some feedback for your player from the coach. They should be providing that during the year to help improvements happen on a continual basis. If your child isn't getting any helpful feedback during the season, speak to the coach and ask for some insight into where your player can improve.

Signing Up for Next Season

You and your child have made it through most the season, dealing with all the ups and downs of club soccer with plenty of time spent on the road and at the field. But before it's even over, it's time to start planning for next year.

TIP

Registration for the following season of play gets underway a few weeks before the end of the current soccer year. You may be asked by the club to signal whether you plan for your child to return by submitting an "intent to play" registration form.

This usually doesn't come with a fee or an ironclad commitment on your part, but knowing where they may have roster gaps if they are losing kids helps the club plan for next year.

REMEMBER

Figuring out roster placements is a jigsaw puzzle for clubs, and where your player is placed for the next season depends not only on your own child's performance but on other factors outside of that. For example, it may be that several players on a higher-level team move to another team or club, opening up spots for others to move up. Or on the flip side, there may not be any openings on a higher-level team.

Should I stay or should I go now?

When looking ahead to next season, the easiest thing to do is to continue with the same club unless you are relocating to a new area. However, before making that call, take the time to consider whether it may be time to make a switch. Here are some areas to focus on when assessing the best next step:

>> **Coaching:** What was your child's experience with their coach? Did the coach help your player improve technically and in game situations? Did they develop a good rapport with the players and team? Was the primary focus on development of the players or results?

Coaching roles for the following season may not be confirmed by the end of the season, but ask if your current coach is expected to stay with the team for next season. If you like the coach and they are expected to stay, that's a very good reason to stick with the current program.

>> **Development:** Did your player improve significantly during the season? The goal of competitive programs is to further the skills and game understanding of every player. Try to assess whether your child's skills and mental understanding of soccer improved throughout the year.

>> **Enjoyment:** Is your child enjoying the experience with the club? This can be impacted by a large number of factors but is ultimately critical to youth soccer working out for them. You shouldn't have to wait until the end of the season to understand this, but it's good to talk the experience through with your child as the year winds down.

If you and your youth player feel comfortable with the situation at your current club, skip to the later section "Returning to your current club." Read on if you want to consider other options.

Trying out for another club

If you want the option of your child moving to another club entirely, the end of season period is the best time to plan for it as clubs often host tryouts before roster spots have been confirmed for the following year.

You can find the dates of tryouts for your child's age group on club websites if they are open for sign-up. The process will likely be similar to the tryout your player went through to join their current club initially. See Chapter 5 for details on this process.

TIP

Reach out to the director of coaching for the club you are trying out at prior to the event via email. A quick note letting them know a bit about your player — their age, position, and drive to perform and contribute to the team — can help introduce them.

Following the tryout, if your child is offered a spot, you'll receive an email with details and a deadline (usually just a few days away) to accept or reject the offer. Because clubs use different terminology for their levels of play, make sure you understand what level the team is at in comparison to your child's current team.

If you feel that a new club is the right way to go for your child, go ahead and accept the offer from the team. You'll soon receive plenty more information on getting to know your new club, likely similar to the process from your previous club.

Returning to your current club

After tryouts have taken place, clubs will send out offers to play-ers to join a specific team. From your existing club, the most likely scenario is that you'll receive an offer to return and play on the same team again. If that's the case and you're comfort-able with the team, you can accept the offer and sit back for next season.

TIP

There may well be turnover on your team that changes its com-plexion significantly for the next season, with players moving up, down, or leaving the club entirely. There may be a new coach as well. So prepare your child that while they're staying with the team, it will likely still be a different experience to some degree.

It's also possible you'll receive an offer for a different team at a higher or lower level. It's not unusual for players to be moved up if the club feels they have the potential to perform at a higher level and there's room on the roster.

Receiving an offer to move up a level (or more)

Getting the news that your club wants your child to move up one or more levels is a good recognition that they feel they have potential to compete and contribute to stronger teams.

It's important to remember that with moving up comes a couple of challenges to consider. Your child will be leaving their teammates — likely their friends — and may not know anyone on their new team unless another player from their current team is moving up with them. This can be a daunting change to prepare for.

REMEMBER

Higher-level teams also usually come with higher expectations regarding the level and intensity of training and performance in games. Playing time may be less equally shared among the play-ers as many teams focus on results and giving more time to what they consider to be the most impactful players. It's worth asking what the playing time expectation is for your player on their new team and to monitor this throughout the season. Although moving up to a higher-level club seems like a win, if they're not actually playing much, their development will stall.

Dealing with moving down or even being cut

There are some conversations that are just going to be hard however well you are prepared for them, and that definitely applies to the discussion when you find out your child has been moved down a level or even cut entirely from the team.

TIP

It's pretty rare in competitive soccer clubs for a child to be completely cut from any team. Player fees are a big part of the club's revenue, and teams generally don't want to lose families. Instead, clubs try to move players around to a different level or even form additional teams if there are multiple players who are best placed at another level of play.

Clubs are also reticent to move players down, though this certainly does often happen. The administrators know taking a step down is emotionally challenging for players and their families to accept, sometimes prompting resentment toward the club. This may make parents and players look for a new team to join, resulting in the club losing a family.

It can certainly be difficult to accept as a parent that your child is being demoted. Parents, of course, are not the best objective judges of their children's performance: They tend to be biased toward them. It may be that your child is not technically, physically, or mentally ready for the level of play they were at (or a combination of these factors).

If they have been given less playing time than others throughout the year, it's a sign that the coach hasn't felt they are able to contribute as much as others. Some coaches also just don't gel with certain players, so a change is necessary for everyone's benefit.

REMEMBER

When a player is moved down, it can be not only a recognition of the fact that they are not at the level of their teammates, but also an opportunity for the player. At a lower level, they may be able to secure more playing time and enjoy being a stronger player on a team more than the challenge of keeping up at a level they may not have been ready for.

Staying Safe Around the Soccer Field

This section is not about injury prevention; see Chapter 7 for that. Instead, this is about how parents can be part of ensuring we have safe environments around youth soccer without any abusive behavior: whether that be physical, emotional, or sexual.

These are difficult topics to discuss, so this guide is drawn directly from advice provided by the experts at the U.S. Center for SafeSport (www.uscenterforsafesport.org). Following is some guidance to questions you may have around ensuring that your child is safe while playing soccer.

What types of abuse do happen in youth sports and soccer?

This is a tough subject to explore, but it's important to recognize that there are a wide range of different types of abuse that do take place:

>> **Sexual abuse:** This type of abuse is described by SafeSport as "The employment, use, persuasion, inducement, enticement, or coercion of a child to engage in, or assist another person to engage in, sexually explicit conduct or sexual exploitation of children, including child pornography."

This type of abuse can include contact and non-contact behaviors, encompassing harassment, sexual exploitation, intentional exposure of private areas, and inappropriate physical conduct.

>> **Physical abuse:** This type of abuse is described by SafeSport as "intentional contact or non-contact behavior that causes, or reasonably threatens to cause, physical harm to another person."

This can also include both contact and non-contact behaviors, such as physical abuse to an athlete or withholding water or nutrition.

>> **Emotional abuse:** These are, according to SafeSport, "behaviors and actions that cause emotional harm to another person."

Examples of such abuse are verbal acts like screaming at, berating, or body-shaming athletes, or stalking or isolating athletes.

Is your child at risk?

SafeSport explains that although we may often assume abusers are strangers to children, the majority of abuse is actually committed by people known to the child and family. In the context of youth soccer, this may include a coach or teammate.

So how can you recognize potentially unsafe environments? Look out for inappropriate behaviors by coaches, including

>> Gift-giving or special treatment given to your child and not the rest of the team

>> Requesting that your child arrives early or stays late on their own

>> Communicating directly to the child without the parent or guardian being included on messages

>> Showing little concern for an athlete's well-being or injuries

>> Punishing the athlete with emotional or physical abuse

Open communication with your child is an effective way to detect any potential abuse or grooming behavior. Kids are often afraid to talk about inappropriate behavior that has happened because they fear they may be blamed or they'll get someone else into trouble.

SafeSport offers these tips to make your child more comfortable expressing concerns to you:

>> Provide your child assurance that they will never get into trouble for talking about anything that makes them uncomfortable and that it will not upset you. Let them know you will always be available to hear anything, and there is no need to be embarrassed. Anything that concerns them or doesn't feel right can be shared.

>> Explain the difference between a "surprise" and a "secret." Surprises are fun and are revealed. If someone is asking them to keep something secret forever, they should share with you what it is because that's not a fun surprise.

What steps should be taken if abuse of a child is suspected?

SafeSport recommends a number of "do's" and "don'ts" if you suspect your child or another child is being abused.

Do:

>> Communicate openly with the child as soon as possible.

>> Remain calm if a child speaks to you about abuse. Let them know you are glad they have shared this information with you, and that they should come to you any time a boundary has been crossed.

>> Document what the child has told you and keep a record of it.

>> Report abuse and reach out to local support providers for assistance.

>> Seek medical attention if necessary for the child.

Don't:

>> Question the child's feelings or ignore them

>> Engage in inappropriate behavior yourself, such as yelling at the coach, an official, or a child

>> Assume the child may just want to stop playing the sport

>> Question whether your child "deserved" any of the treatment

These do's and don'ts are a very general guide. SafeSport also offers much more detailed guidance for each age group on its website (www.uscenterforsafesport.org). If you suspect abuse, you should immediately report it to your child's youth soccer club leadership or appropriate authorities.

IN THIS CHAPTER

» **Eating the right nutrients**

» **Getting in shape for soccer**

» **Coping with injuries**

» **Taking care of concussion risks**

» **Focusing on mental wellness**

Chapter **7**

Staying Healthy and Handling Injuries

S occer is a great way for youth athletes to get and stay in shape, and playing has mental health pluses, too. Being in good condition for soccer can help lead to a healthier lifestyle overall with long-term benefits into adulthood. In this chapter, you find out what to eat, drink, and do to be fit for the game.

Like any sport, especially a contact sport with a lot of movement, player injuries are bound to happen. These can range from minor contusions to serious knee or head injuries. There's no way to prevent all injuries, but this chapter covers some ways to mitigate risk and explains what to do when injury does occur, with a special focus on handling the tricky case of concussions.

Managing Nutrition

"Eat well, play well" is a mantra you may want to encourage in your youth soccer player. A good, nutritious diet will certainly aid health and good physical development, which can help with performance as a soccer player. After all, soccer legend Cristiano Ronaldo once said, "Good nutrition is the core of my success."

Food is fuel for the body, and getting the right nutrients — particularly the right balance of proteins, carbohydrates, and fats — can help provide the strong energy levels for good athletic performance as well as contribute to a positive diet overall. Eating right is about being thoughtful about long-term nutrition for your child along with helping them get the energy needed from positive short-term nutrition choices on game day itself.

TIP

Younger kids (under 10) play shorter matches and don't burn through as much energy as older kids playing longer games on bigger fields, so your focus on diet will need to increase as your child moves up through the age groups.

REMEMBER

Just as important as fueling performance, good nutrition habits can lead to a much healthier existence in general beyond the soccer field. Instilling good habits in your child at a young age can much improve health prospects and the likelihood of long-term health and wellness.

This section explores some of the fundamentals of good nutrition that all kids should follow for a healthy lifestyle as well as some specific tips for aiding soccer performance, given the demands of the game physically.

Fueling up for the field

Playing soccer burns through calories quickly, so it's key to prepare the body with the right fuel to play and stay strong throughout practices and especially matches, particularly during tournament weekends, where your kid may play multiple times in a day.

Getting ready to play actually starts the day before. A meal with starchy foods and plenty of protein the night prior to getting on the field provides fuel that can be ready to burn the next day.

On game day itself, a light meal a couple of hours before playing will set a base of necessary calories to burn during the match. Carbohydrates like bread, rice, or pasta are the simplest way to stock up the body. Protein, such as chicken or tofu, also provides plenty of energy. A side of vegetables is also a good idea to add necessary nutrients.

Hydrating before and during playing is critical for the body, but make sure these fluids are not too sugary or full of caffeine, which can lead to crashes. Water and low-sugar sports drinks are a good way to get hydrated to play. Plain water is enough most of the time, though there are some advantages to sports drinks with added electrolytes and potassium.

TIP

Don't load your kid up with a big, heavy meal before they get onto the pitch. Playing soccer requires feeling light on your feet, so a greasy, fatty, or overly large meal can lead to discomfort and feelings of sluggishness while playing.

As well as meals, snacking the right way is an important way to stay fueled up. This is particularly true during tournaments, when your child may play multiple games in a day with only a short break in between — not enough time for a full meal to be digested.

Avoid sugary snacks and try to pack a few options that provide some fast and healthy nutrition, such as the following:

>> **Fruits:** Bananas, apples, and oranges are traditional staples of fresh refreshment.

>> **Bars:** Granola bars and protein bars can provide a variety of nutrients, though be sure to check that they aren't packed with too much sugar.

>> **Other snacks:** Graham crackers and plain bagels provide quick carbs to fuel up.

Bring a small cooler to the field, especially if it's a tournament day and your child has multiple matches. This will allow you to keep drinks and snacks nice and cool — as well as being neatly in one place!

Post-game

Replenishing the body after playing helps to rebuild muscle and restore energy. A quick snack within 45 minutes of the final whistle is helpful, followed by a full meal packed with protein, healthy fats, and carbs to truly refuel.

Continuing to hydrate in the first hour after playing is also important. Water is the simplest option, but sports drinks with added electrolytes can aid the body's recovery, especially after playing in hot conditions and perspiring a lot. Coconut water provides electrolytes as well, while a smoothie laced with added protein powder can provide carbohydrates and proteins for muscle recovery as well as fluid replenishment.

Food and drinks to avoid

Not eating the wrong foods is just as important as eating the right foods. It probably won't shock you that greasy, fried, fatty fast-food meals provide little in the way of helpful nutrition and a lot in the way of harm to the body if eaten too often, slowing down performance.

Food and drinks packed with added sugar are also bad for the body, leading to weight gain and energy crashes.

As a general rule, whole foods — including grains, vegetables, and plenty of fruit — are a much better choice for both athletic performance and general health than processed foods filled with preservatives and artificial ingredients.

Especially when traveling to soccer tournaments, stopping for fast food can be hard to avoid. But if possible, do skip the fast-food option prior to playing in games. And remember, if eating while on the road at some point, many fast-food places now have some healthy choices — and there's no need to super-size every part of the meal, which only loads on more empty calories.

WARNING

Energy drinks, though increasingly popular, can be dangerous for children and adolescents and should be avoided. They often contain large amounts of caffeine, which can prompt headaches, irregular heartbeats, and issues sleeping. In addition, they are often loaded with sugar and other questionable ingredients and chemicals.

TIP

It's not very realistic to expect your child to have a perfect, whole-foods-only diet all the time. In fact, allowing or encouraging some consumption of treats is a perfectly fine part of a balanced overall diet.

Working with Fitness Programs

Soccer's a sport where fitness plays a key role in being able to perform well on the field: It's an endurance sport that even in high-level youth soccer can see players running several miles a game. Speed, strength, and agility are also critical to performing well in game situations to outpace or hold off opponents and quickly change direction with the fast-moving ball.

So, it certainly makes sense to focus on good fitness for your youth soccer player, especially as they grow into puberty and play at more advanced, competitive levels.

Fitness for under-12s

When considering focusing on additional fitness training outside of playing soccer, make sure that it's appropriate for your child's age. Children under the age of 12 really shouldn't need any specific fitness-focused training outside of a good range of playing outside and taking part in sports.

Pushing your child to run a bunch of laps and do push-ups at a young age is likely to be both a miserable experience for the child and counterproductive in encouraging them to enjoy and seek out physical exercise.

Instead, especially for younger children, a variety of fun games and exercises they enjoy and want to engage in is the best way to seed a lifetime of sporting enjoyment and develop athletic skills.

Simply running around the playground and playing tag a few times a week builds stamina, speed, and general fitness levels — and is fun for your kid (whereas trying to make them run laps around a field is, well, not fun or something they'll want to do frequently).

REMEMBER

Playing on a jungle gym, climbing around and jumping, and going to a trampoline park are great cardiovascular exercises that raise heart rates and build agility, balance, and explosive-ness without kids even thinking about it. All of those things are helpful on the soccer field, but they're all free and enjoyable with friends. There's no need for dedicated fitness drills for a 9-year-old.

Once your child reaches the teenage years, especially if your child is playing competitive soccer, there is value in focusing more specifically on fitness drills outside of the soccer field, so read on if your child is ready to try some additional exercises.

REMEMBER

Playing additional sports can be continued from childhood through adolescence and has many extra fitness benefits. For more on this, see Chapter 9.

The benefits of fitness training for teenagers

There's plenty of debate about the value of fitness programs outside of soccer training. Some people argue that time is better spent solely on developing skills on the soccer field. There's no doubt that the majority of a competitive soccer player's time dedicated to the sport should be spent with the ball at their feet to develop mastery of it.

That said, adding fitness training to your child's athletic development in adolescence can allow them to better deploy key core soccer skills. Fitness training makes kids faster to the ball, better conditioned to perform at peak ability throughout a long match, and stronger in challenges for the ball. Improving core physical performance can also provide better conditioning to maximize the possibilities of injury prevention.

For kids in their teenage years, the following are some simple areas to focus on and drills that develop core athletic conditioning for soccer.

Cardio

While it may seem like running long distances is good conditioning for soccer, remember that most running in soccer is typically short and explosive (speed-focused), and involves quick changes of direction. The pacing of slow, multi-mile runs in one direction doesn't necessarily translate to the soccer field.

Instead, short shuttle runs of 15–20 yards are an easy drill to set up between cones on any playing field. Players race to one cone and then back as fast as possible. Side-to-side and backward running can also be added.

These sprints can be repeated around 15 times with breaks of 30 to 60 seconds in between each run.

REMEMBER Around 90 percent of runs in soccer are less than 30 yards, so training for speed over short distances — and the stamina to repeat those runs — is more important than running long distances.

Strength

Hitting the gym and bulking up may seem the easiest way to add strength, but care should be taken in weight training, especially for growing adolescents. Moreover, simply adding bicep or tricep muscle isn't necessarily the most effective type of strength training for soccer. However, developing core strength not only can allow for greater ability to shield and win the ball, but it can also help prevent injury.

A good way to start building strength that can quickly impact performance is to focus on plyometrics, which builds explosive power. This can include exercises such as burpees, box jumps, or squat jumps.

Core strength and stability can also be built with exercises such as planking, crunches, and leg lifts. Upper body strength can be developed with pull-ups and push-ups.

Agility

Playing soccer involves a lot of quick turns, so being able to change direction rapidly — accelerating and decelerating — while staying balanced dramatically enhances performance on the field.

Simple agility training can be performed at home with cones or ladders on the ground, with your player rapidly weaving in and out. Short shuttle runs or sprinting in zigzag patterns are also easy ways to improve agility.

TIP

Every child is different. The biggest gains can be made where your child may lag in one particular area, such as adding speed or strength. But remember, adolescents grow at different rates, so your child may only be one natural growth spurt away from changing physically at a rapid speed regardless of any training.

Tackling Injuries

Injury, unfortunately, is inevitable for any soccer player. The type and severity of injuries varies widely as does the range of appropriate treatments and rest periods. I explore some of the more common injuries here, look at some injury prevention tips, and examine how to plan for speedy and complete recoveries.

REMEMBER

During games and practices, it's the responsibility of the adult leading the play to stop the game if a child is injured on the field. During a game, this responsibility falls to the referee and during practices, to the team coach. While it can be hard to see your child get injured on the pitch and your instinct — especially when they are younger — may be to run out to them, the immediate responsibility to stop play and check on the child's well-being belongs to the referee and coach.

TIP

Most coaches have a lot of experience seeing injuries take place on the field — likely a lot more than you have. It's important to trust their ability to recognize the severity of an injury. Children are, of course, emotional, and it's common to see a child in tears over a minor injury that isn't serious and within minutes feel fine and be back on the field. Conversely, coaches typically recognize when an injury is actually serious, such as the risk of concussion from a head injury (see the later section "Figuring Out Concussion Protocols)."

If a player has an injury that results in a stoppage of play, it's usual practice for the child to leave the field and a substitute to come on. In the unlikely event of a serious injury, at that point the coach may ask the parent to come over to assess the severity and take care of the player. If an injury requires immediate medical treatment, check to see whether there are medical services available onsite — this is likely the case at tournament events but not at all individual matches or practices.

REMEMBER

In most cases, for less serious injuries, the player will rest on the sideline and then return to play when they feel comfortable, subbing back in for another player. If the injury does not require immediate medical treatment but does mean they can't continue to play — such as from a minor twisted ankle injury — they may remain on the subs bench for the rest of the game cheering on their teammates.

TIP

It's common practice in youth soccer for all the players on the field to kneel down on one leg when another player is injured and play has been stopped. This is done to show sympathy for the player and to pause everyone in place so coaches and the referee can focus on handling the injury and not worry about the rest of the players moving around or trying to tend to their teammate.

Contusions and minor injuries

While there are no "good" injuries, there will often be times when your kid gets a minor injury that may require only a brief break from play and some basic treatment at home.

The following sections cover some of the most common minor injuries and treatments.

Bruises

Getting whacked on the legs or having someone step on your feet is a very common occurrence in soccer. Contusions are painful and cause swelling.

While painful, bruises typically heal fast. As well as pain relief medication that can help manage pain and reduce inflammation, the infamous "RICE" method is easy to remember and deploy:

>> **Rest:** Resting can avoid further bruising.

>> **Ice:** Apply ice via an ice pack or cold compress to numb the area and reduce swelling. Apply every 20 minutes after the injury for the first few hours or longer as needed.

>> **Compression:** Apply a bandage to press down on the injured area and reduce swelling.

>> **Elevation:** Rest the injured limb above the level of the heart, which also reduces swelling.

Blisters

Those nasty little injuries on the feet are very uncomfortable, making it hard to continue playing. A sore, red area on the foot can quickly expand to a bubble sac of fluid that can become painful.

Blisters occur due to friction between the foot and the footwear and generally shouldn't occur if the player has the correct sized shoes. New cleats can also cause blisters: It's best to break them in before playing by doing some light walking or jogging in them for a day or two before wearing them in practice or a match.

To treat a blister, first of all make sure it's covered up with a bandage or dressing to prevent more abrasion on it. If there's a large sac of fluid, it can be drained carefully by puncturing with a sterile needle. Now be sure to keep the blister area clean and apply some antiseptic. Avoid further friction by staying away from soccer or other activities that could cause further friction until it's healed, which usually takes up to a week.

Abrasions

Scrapes from falling or sliding on the playing surface can easily scrape a layer of skin away. Rough and hard grass surfaces or artificial surfaces can exacerbate the abrasion. These can be painful and lead to bleeding.

In most cases, these are just surface-level wounds that can be treated by cleaning them up at home with soap and water and applying some antiseptic. The abrasion should then be dressed to cover it up. These steps are important to prevent infection, which can cause further complications. It should heal within a week or two. If the wound instead shows more redness or pus, there may be an infection and medical treatment should be sought to clear it up.

Strains and sprains

Strains, sprains, and injuries to soft tissue are common in soccer and are usually minor though severe cases can result in extended time on the sidelines.

Muscle or tendon injuries occur when they are overextended or subject to excessive force that causes a tear or excessive strain. Sudden movement in soccer can cause this, especially if the athlete is fatigued, with muscles such as the hamstring, calf, and groin particularly susceptible.

Sprains often manifest with bruising and swelling. In soccer, ankle sprains are particularly common due to the twists and turns of the sport or due to contact from another player.

Initial treatment for strains and sprains can follow the RICE approach (see the earlier section "Bruises") to reduce swelling and allow the body to heal.

REMEMBER

Sprains or strains can be mild or serious. If the RICE method isn't proving effective, you may need to seek medical attention for a proper recovery from a more serious strain or sprain that has torn a muscle or tendon.

Suffering serious injury and recovering

Unfortunately, soccer is a contact sport with players moving at rapid speeds and often colliding into each other that can result in injuries. In addition, the strain on the body from the quick turns and sudden movements can result in severe muscle or ligament tears.

For what to do in the case of head injuries, see "Figuring Out Concussion Protocols" later in this chapter.

Knee injuries

For the soccer player, the knee is one of the most common parts of the body that can be impacted by the twists and turns of soccer or sudden impact, resulting in pain and swelling. These injuries include ACL (anterior cruciate ligament) or meniscus (cartilage) tears. These tears may require surgery depending on the seriousness of the tear. Your medical professional can advise of you of the necessary action and recovery process, which takes many months.

Studies have shown that female players are more susceptible to ACL injuries, though the cause of this isn't entirely understood. Some experts suggest additional strength and plyometric training can help reduce the risk of ACL tears. See "Working with Fitness Programs" earlier in this chapter for some suggested training routines.

Fractures and dislocations

Especially for teenage players, the impacts in playing soccer from collisions or falls can result in broken bones and dislocated joints that can be very painful and require substantial recovery time. Leg and feet bones are particularly susceptible to fractures, including the tibia and fibula in the former and the metatarsal in the latter. Recovery may include surgery, immobilization for several weeks, and physical therapy, a process that can often take several months.

If your child suffers a serious injury, be aware that this is not only a physical issue but also a mental challenge. They may miss a substantial part of the season and be concerned about issues including recovering fully from injury and returning to reclaim their place on the team.

TIP

Reassure your child that, unfortunately, serious injuries do happen to most soccer players at some stage. Coaches understand that this happens and that young bodies can make full recoveries.

Recovering from injury

If there's one thing that can make us feel old as parents, it's seeing how rapidly children (especially at younger ages) can recover from injury.

However, don't be fooled by your child's desire to get back on the field as soon as possible — while minor injuries will heal fast, it's very important to allow any serious injuries to fully heal before your child returns to the soccer field (or other physical activities that may be impacted). Coming back to the field too soon risks a reoccurrence of the same injury and further extended time on the sidelines.

REMEMBER

Once children reach puberty and grow into full-sized bodies, the risk of severe injury increases rapidly. Impacts on the field between teenagers can result in much more significant blows to the body than between lighter, younger children. The strain on muscles and tendons is also much more significant.

Knee injuries are generally the most common serious injuries for soccer players. The stress of rapid turns and twists at high speeds can result in ligament damage that varies from minor to severe, including season-ending injury that may take many months or even longer to heal. If knee injuries persist, be sure to see a specialist sports doctor for advice.

Preventing injury

While nothing can prevent injury happening at some point, your child can follow some basic steps to minimize some of the risks.

These steps get more important as youth soccer players age; after puberty strikes, the risk of serious injury increases considerably.

Many preventative strategies are already covered in this book by preparing your kid to play in the right way: This includes getting the right size footwear, staying hydrated and following a good diet, practicing good technique with the ball, and engaging in additional strength and agility training that can strengthen muscles and improve flexibility.

It's also important to warm up and cool down before each game, following stretching exercises the team's coach should teach. In addition, especially in later teenage years when the intensity of games and practice increases, it's important to rest and recover between sessions.

TIP

If your child is going through an intense period of training and matches, ask whether they are feeling fatigued and remind them to listen to their body. Pushing through fatigue, pain, or soreness can risk injury and do more harm than good.

Figuring Out Concussion Protocols

A concussion is a traumatic brain injury, usually caused (especially in soccer) by a blow to the head. Concussions impact regular brain function, with symptoms such as headaches, dizziness, and nausea common. While a single concussion is typically neither life-threatening nor likely to have a permanent impact on the brain, the effect can be serious and last for days, weeks, or even months.

WARNING

The long-term consequences of multiple concussion injuries can be extremely serious.

Back in the years when little was known about the seriousness of head injuries and the long-term risks of concussion, soccer players — including kids of all ages — repeatedly headed heavy leather balls. Relatively little heed was paid to blows to the head, with players often continuing after taking a heavy knock there from an elbow or another player's head.

Fortunately, all of this has changed in recent years. Balls have become lighter, but more importantly, kids under the age of 10 are not permitted to head balls in games or practices. This not only reduces the risk of injury from repeated heading of the ball, but also the risk of heads clashing if two players try to head the ball at the same time.

In addition, protocols around addressing blows to the head during games have become far more serious as have how possible or actual concussions are handled by officials and coaches. Some states mandate sports coaches to take concussion training courses.

TIP

Check that the club your child is playing for has a written concussion protocol. This should lay out guidelines for parents and coaches to provide clarity on the process to be followed around any head injury.

Here are some best practices clubs typically follow:

>> **Educate and inform:** It's important that everyone involved with the club — especially coaches and parents — understand what concussions are and that strict protocols must be followed. Sharing this information via club communication channels and coach-parent meetings can ensure that a shared approach to following concussion protocols is in place.

>> **Safety first:** "If in doubt, take the player out" is a mantra many teams use following a head injury. Removing a player from the field if they show any signs or symptoms of a concussion is the safest way to address the situation. Concussion symptoms may not even appear for hours after any incident.

>> **Medical clearance:** If a player has a suspected concussion, they should not return to play until a medical professional has provided clearance that it is safe to do so. Parents or coaches should never make this decision on their own.

Recovering from a Concussion

Being cleared to play after a concussion doesn't mean returning immediately to resume full training and match programs. It's crucial that a step-by-step process, adhering to professional medical guidance, is followed for returning to play. Check with your medical professional for the right steps, but as a general guide you can expect multiple stages of recovery:

>> **Rest:** For the first couple of days after injury, players should completely rest both physically and mentally.

>> **Light activity:** For the next couple of days, as symptoms are subsiding, 10–15 minutes of aerobic activity such as walking or stationary bike exercise is advised.

>> **Moderate activity:** The next step is to introduce some slightly more intense jogging or stationary biking that raises the heart rate and starts some more body and head movement.

>> **Non-contact drills:** After a couple of weeks, it's time to engage in some more intense movement, which can include sprinting and soccer-specific drills such as dribbling around cones or shooting. However, there should still be no contact or activity with other players.

>> **Resume practice and games:** Following a week or two of non-contact drills, a return to normal practice, including contact, can take place in preparation for returning to game play.

As your child progresses through each stage, watch closely for any signs of concussion symptoms. If they continue or return at any stage, cease activity and consult your medical professional. Only move on to the next stage of recovery if the symptoms are subsiding.

WARNING

The seriousness of a head injury can be hard to understand compared to many other injuries. Bruises and swelling take place inside the skull rather than visibly on a limb and don't impact physical abilities immediately in the same way as, say, a sprained or broken ankle does. But the long-term impact of a head injury can be devastating, and plenty of care needs to be taken before any return to the soccer field.

If your child has had a concussion in the past or receives a head injury outside of soccer activities, be sure to inform your player's coach so that they are aware of it.

Recognizing the Importance of Mental Health and Performance

Before we dive into topics of mental health and performance for youth soccer players, note that this section just provides general advice about the mental approach to playing soccer. For any mental health emergency, immediately call 9-8-8 to reach the Suicide and Crisis Lifeline or go to the nearest emergency room. Your state may also have its own crisis helpline (search Google for your state) and these lifelines are available 24/7.

In this section, you explore mental health with respect to performing and how to prioritize wellness for the youth soccer player.

Understanding mental wellness

Our emotional, psychological, and social well-being are at the core of our mental health. This drives many aspects of our everyday existence: how we behave, make decisions, handle stress, and empathize with others.

Much of this book focuses on the physical activity of soccer and the benefits of being physically healthy, fit, and having the right diet. Ensuring that you are paying as much attention to the mental wellness along with the physical wellness of your child as a youth soccer player is just as important.

Challenges with mental health are far from unusual for any adult or child, impacting one in six children. Mental illness often goes undiagnosed and untreated, and while varying significantly in severity, can impact functioning in everyday life as well as physical health.

In the past, young athletes have often been expected to "push through" the mental challenges of playing soccer or other sports. This can lead to increased feelings of anxiety and stress, and exacerbate mental health challenges.

REMEMBER

It's increasingly recognized that, as swimming legend Michael Phelps put it, "It's okay not to be okay." This understanding is important to remove any stigma around athletes speaking about and addressing mental health challenges.

Rather than prioritizing "toughness," many experts now recommend focusing on mental wellness and a flexible approach to understanding the challenges of growing up and playing youth sports — using the positives of sport to develop confidence and deal emotionally with challenges.

Managing expectations

Whether knowingly or not, parents often set expectations that are unrealistic for their child to achieve. This can lead to the child feeling disappointment, as if they have failed both themselves and you. If you tell your child they are the best athlete out there and should be dominating, you're setting them up to fail — even the greatest athletes have ups and downs.

TIP

Develop age-appropriate goals that focus on and reward personal growth, strong effort, and enjoyment of the sport. At the younger ages, the expectation going to any soccer practice or game should be to enjoy it — not indexing in on performance or results.

Focusing on the outcome — winning a match, scoring a goal, or saving every shot — sets a goal your child can't achieve every time. Setting expectations that they will work hard, give their all to support the team, and deploy the skills they have learned through practicing will encourage successful performance.

If your child becomes focused on binary targets that may not even be in their control — making it onto the roster of an elite team or being the top scorer on the team — they are setting themselves up for disappointment. Realistic goals that build on what they are working to develop as a person and a player can be both achievable and positive. For example, ask your child what they have been focusing on in practice and improving at. Then set a goal to perform that skill in an upcoming match.

Accomplishing something the coach and player have been focused on that doesn't depend on anything but their own effort and implementation can bring a great sense of reward and encourage good practice habits.

Your child is only one player on a team of many. Remind them they can't control every aspect of the team's performance or result. Focusing on what they can control — their own effort, their own attitude, their own preparation and goals for each game — can give them a positive sense of what they can achieve.

Keeping soccer in perspective and staying calm

A serious youth soccer player's life can often feel like it is revolving around the field, with multiple practices and games a week. It's important to help prevent your child from feeling like games and their performances make or break their week. Encouraging other activities and taking intentional breaks from soccer are key to maintaining balance.

Immediately after a game, don't focus on the score or spend the car ride analyzing your kid's performance. Focusing right away on that only adds to the mental burden of the game and doesn't allow your child to reset and breathe. Leave it a day before talking about a game, especially after a disappointing result, unless your child does need comfort in the interim. Every child is different, but the important thing is for them not to feel like what has happened should be consuming them after the game.

If your child is feeling anxious about soccer, work with them on strategies to stay calm. This can be helped by getting away from the soccer field and taking a break from the sport for a few days. Getting out into nature is a proven way to help reset the body and mind. At home, deep and slow breathing exercises can be helpful.

Struggling with soccer

Burnout is real. Competitive soccer puts considerable demands on any young player, with a long rotation of games, tournaments, team practices, and extra practices.

Make sure that you are talking to your child about their experience in the sport and listen for signs of exhaustion and frustration. Let them feel like they can speak to you freely about the challenges they may be having.

TIP

Sometimes it's helpful to remind your child that playing soccer is a choice. It is something that they can stop doing or take a break from if they need to. They may feel that because much of their life revolves around it and their family has invested a lot into their soccer, they have to keep playing. They may likely choose to continue. But understanding that it's an activity they don't *have* to do can help break a feeling of being locked to the sport.

For some players, the workload of competitive soccer may be too much. Instead of an all-or-nothing approach, remind them they can play instead at recreational levels. Or if they are playing both club and school soccer, consider choosing one instead of a double load.

REMEMBER

Speak to your child's coach if you feel they are suffering from burnout. A good coach will have strategies and tactics they can employ to help the player and support them to work through the challenges, reassuring the child that they have a broad network supporting them and understanding what they are going through.

Chapter **8**

Goalkeeping Is Different

O ne player on each team wears a contrasting uniform from everyone else. One player is allowed to use their hands. One player is different — the goalkeeper.

Goalkeepers need different skills, different equipment, different training, and even a different mindset than their teammates. And for parents, it can mean a nerve-wracking time as their child is peppered with shots on goal.

If your child gravitates toward goalkeeping, tasked with the responsibility of stopping the ball from going into the back of the net, this chapter gives you all you need to know.

Mastering Goalkeeping Basics

Goalkeeping is a specialized position requiring the development of skills that are very different from outfield players. It'll be helpful for you to understand some of the basics that your child should learn as they go on their journey as a goalkeeper.

REMEMBER

Yes, goalkeepers can use their hands — but only within their own penalty area! This is a key distinction: Otherwise, goalkeepers would be wandering up the field using their hands to catch and throw the ball (which would make soccer much more like America's version of football). If they handle the ball outside their own penalty area, they'll be penalized just like any other player.

The place where goalkeepers can handle the ball, the *penalty area*, is marked out as a rectangular box. This varies in size depending on the age group your kid is playing in, getting larger just as the whole field itself does for older age groups.

TIP

Being tall is a natural advantage as a goalkeeper, since it's obviously easier to reach the ball with more height. But for a youth player, being shorter than other players shouldn't stop anyone from trying their hand (pun intended!) at goalkeeping.

For a start, how relatively tall a kid is at the age of 10 doesn't necessarily indicate how tall they'll be when they are older — growth spurts can happen at all sorts of ages. But more importantly, kids can enjoy the position whatever their height and excel at it even if they aren't the tallest on the block. Picking up the core skills described here will go a long way to success protecting the net.

REMEMBER

The first time your child goes in goal in recreational soccer, they may not know very much about what they're doing or how to save the ball. That's okay! If they enjoy it and move on to more competitive levels, there'll be plenty of time to pick up the needed skills.

Making saves

Stopping shots by the opposition team from going into the goal is the main focus for any goalkeeper. This is primarily done by stopping the ball with use of the hands, though any body part will do to block a shot, and some goalkeepers are famous for saving shots with their feet. The key is to have the reflexes to react quickly and get hands or feet to the ball and deflect it away from the goal.

The most spectacular saves come when goalkeepers dive for the ball. This looks exactly like it sounds: The goalkeeper launches themselves into the air to try and reach a ball they couldn't otherwise get to without leaping. This skill requires plenty of athleticism as well as a fearless attitude. It takes time for any young goalkeeper to learn to dive effectively.

TIP

An important key to good shot-stopping is getting into a good position to have the best chance of reaching the ball. This actually means the goalkeeper's use of their feet — in the form of nimble footwork and quickly moving to the right spot — are just as important as the hands for the goalkeeper. Helpful coaching for a goalkeeper should have a large focus on positioning and footwork.

An even better result for a goalkeeper and their team than simply deflecting the ball away is when they can gather or catch the ball to claim control of it. Simply deflecting the ball away with a save may mean it goes back to the opposition, while getting hold of the ball gives the goalkeeper's team possession and the potential to launch a counterattack.

REMEMBER

Goalkeepers can punch the ball as well as grab or push it with their hands. Sometimes this can be the most effective way to get the ball a good distance away from the goal to safety. Goalkeepers do need to be careful not to strike an opponent when they punch the ball.

Distributing the ball

Flashy saves catch the eye for goalkeepers, but a less obvious element of play can be just as important for contributing to the team performance — getting the ball quickly and accurately to teammates.

There are two main ways goalkeepers are tasked with trying to distribute the ball. The first is from a goal kick, when play is restarted after the opposition has kicked the ball out of play over the goal line.

Goalkeepers then usually kick the ball, which cannot be moving when struck, back into play. I say "usually" because it's not actually required for the goalkeeper to take a goal kick — technically, any player on the team can do it. But it's normally the goalkeeper because they are positioned behind everyone else on the field. Goal kicks can be passed a short distance to a teammate nearby or booted hard up the field to try and launch an attack.

The second way a goalkeeper can distribute the ball is after they have caught it or gathered it from the ground. Unlike from a goal kick, the ball doesn't have to be static when kicked — and in fact, it doesn't have to be kicked at all. The goalkeeper can use their hands to throw or roll the ball to a teammate, which can be a quick and effective way to distribute the ball.

Alternately, the goalkeeper can try to launch the ball down the field by drop-kicking it. This involves the goalkeeper dropping the ball and then punting it with their foot. Ideally, the ball goes all the way into the opposition's half of the field.

TIP

Kicking the ball a long way down the field from a goal kick or by punting it can be difficult for youth goalkeepers, especially at younger ages. To do it well requires both power and the ability to loft the ball into the air, which is not an easy skill to master. It is important to try to improve this skill since weak kicks can easily turn the ball straight back over to the opposition close to the goal and cause a shooting chance.

Communicating with the team

It may look like the goalkeeper is on an island from the rest of the team, standing behind everyone else and largely restricted to roaming the penalty area in front of the goal. But in fact, the goalkeeper is one of the most important players in organizing the team — and especially the defensive unit. Because the goalkeeper roams behind all of their teammates, they have a good view of impending attacks and can help move players into the right positions to be best positioned defensively.

TIP

Goalkeepers need to loudly communicate with their teammates to make sure they get out of the way when they are leaping to grab a ball. This is done by calling out "keeper's ball" loudly to make it clear the goalkeeper will claim it.

Communication skills are important to develop as a goalkeeper, especially at more competitive levels. The goalkeeper needs to be able to understand the game well tactically and can help position players ahead to the team's advantage. This is essentially done by yelling at defenders to tell them where to go! Think of the goalkeeper as an on-field general, organizing the troops.

This type of communication can be intimidating for some players and challenging for parents to encourage. After all, we often tell our children not to be bossy. But that's really what is required in the goalkeeping position! So it's important to let your kid know it's okay to be loud and commanding as a goalkeeper, and in fact, it's beneficial to the team.

REMEMBER

Strong vocal chords are obviously an advantage here. If your child isn't naturally loud and doesn't enjoy telling people what to do, the more competitive levels of soccer may be challenging as a goalkeeper. On the other hand, goalkeeper training emphasizes these elements, so it can be a good way for kids to learn leadership and communication skills.

Concentrating in goal

Watching your child play goalkeeper can in itself be an exercise in patience. There can often be long stretches of play where the ball doesn't go anywhere near their goal, so the goalkeeper is often isolated from anything happening. For the goalkeeper themselves, even more than you, this can be one of the biggest challenges.

All of a sudden, there may be a quick attack from the other team and the goalkeeper must be ready to jump into action. Being able to hold concentration is a key challenge, and as we know, children aren't always the most patient! This is also a reminder that goalkeeping is not for every personality, but it can also be a great way to develop good concentration skills. Goalkeepers concentrating well on the action will be playing with their head up observing at all times.

TIP

Everyone's concentration lapses from time to time and it's hard to expect young children to be any different! Mistakes shouldn't be chastised, especially immediately after a game.

Keeping Up with Goalkeeping Equipment

Goalkeepers not only have a different role from everyone else on their team, but they also need to look different and require some specialized equipment. This does come at an extra cost, though it's fairly reasonable compared to goaltenders in ice hockey, for example. Read on for what you'll need to get.

Jerseys

Because special rules apply to goalkeepers that don't apply to the rest of their team — they can handle the ball in their own penalty area, for example — they need to be easily identified. This means that they wear a different, contrasting color jersey distinct from their teammates. For example, if all of their team is wearing red jerseys, they'll wear a color such as blue, yellow, or green rather than red (or a similar color, like pink).

Goalkeepers also often wear long-sleeved jerseys. This can help provide a bit more protection from abrasion as the keeper is often landing on the ground after diving to stop the ball. Goalkeeper jerseys boast extra padding around the elbow area to provide further protection.

If your kid's goalkeeper jersey doesn't come with built-in padding, you can purchase specific elbow pads to place underneath.

Shorts and pants

Although outfield players must wear shorts, goalkeepers can choose whether they wear shorts or long pants. This comes down to personal preference — in hotter climates, it may be a bit uncomfortable to wear long pants, for example. That said, pants can provide a bit more protection when sliding on the ground to try to stop or grab the ball.

Goalkeeper shorts or pants also usually feature extra padding for protection down each side and on the knees (in the case of pants). They are also differently colored than their outfield teammates' shorts.

Make sure all of your kid's goalkeeping clothing fits comfortably. Goalkeepers need to be flexible, so anything too tight that restricts movement hurts performance, while anything too loose risks getting snagged.

Gloves

Perhaps the most important element of the goalkeepers' wardrobe is gloves. These aren't worn to stay warm; they are heavily padded to protect delicate fingers and thumbs from the impact of the ball, which can be critical to prevent injuries.

Gloves also cushion the impact of the ball and make it easier to grip and hold the ball. The palm of the glove is the key element here; usually made of a latex material, the surface helps the "stickiness" of the glove to grip the ball. Keep an eye on the condition of this part of the glove in particular. It wears out fastest as the ball strikes the palm most often, and the gloves need to be replaced when the surface becomes rough and loses its stickiness.

The fingers are also very important, protecting those small digits from harm when struck with the ball. Goalkeeper gloves often have small plastic inserts in each finger to help provide extra protection and firmness.

There are several styles of cuts for goalkeeper gloves. Take the time to measure your child's hand and see which cuts are the most comfortable. Go to a goalkeeper glove website for instructions on measuring your kid's hand and the different cut styles.

TIP

Good goalkeeper gloves are a worthwhile investment. Not only do they provide more protection and grip for your goalkeeping child, they are also likely to be more durable and last longer — probably paying for the extra dollars in the long run. An excellent pair of goalkeeper gloves can be purchased for around $50. This is an item you will need to purchase separately for your kid — it won't be provided as part of the team uniform.

Shin guards

Goalkeepers need to protect their shins just like outfield players do, so this piece of equipment is the same (see Chapter 1 for an overview).

Looking at Specialized Training Programs

In competitive programs, goalkeepers usually receive specialized training in sessions separate from the rest of the team. These sessions are led by dedicated goalkeeping coaches, almost always former goalkeepers who understand the technical, mental, and physical parts of the game that are unique to the position.

The volume of specialized and separated training varies by team, but usually there are one or two sessions per week. This is typically done by grouping together goalkeepers across various teams at a club at a similar age, which may mean your kid is practicing with kids of varied abilities.

Be sure to see if there is a dedicated program director for goalkeeping at the club if you're playing at a competitive level. This is a good sign that the club is seriously invested in this area and provides the goalkeeping coaches solid direction and training.

Ideally these specialized training sessions should also mean there is a good ratio of coach to kids, allowing for the type of personalized support goalkeepers do typically need. If there are around six kids to each goalkeeping coach, then you can feel confident your kid is getting good attention each practice.

Proper training can teach young goalkeepers the best technical ways to dive for a ball and collapse on the ball effectively and safely.

Goalkeeper coaches often have a slightly more direct approach than team coaches. They have a single-minded focus on developing one position, and an important part of goalkeeping is developing strong, vocal personalities. So goalkeeping coaches themselves usually have strong vocal personalities, and this shows in how they handle their sessions.

As your child advances in goalkeeping programs, look for more specialized skills to come into focus. When exploring programs, see if they have specific plans for developing key areas of goalkeeping such as

>> **Shot-stopping:** Training should focus on a variety of ways to save the ball, such as dives, quick reflex stops, and ground-level blocks.

>> **Positioning:** Understanding how to position the body to create more difficult angles for attackers to shoot at and where to stand in relation to the goal.

>> **Footwork:** Learning to be light on the feet and quickly reposition laterally to get in the right position to make a save or catch a cross.

>> **Crosses:** Working on the goalkeeper's ability to catch or punch the ball away when it is launched high into the penalty area by the attacking team.

>> **Distribution:** An important part of the goalkeeper's role is to get the ball quickly and accurately to teammates. Drills

should focus on kicking the ball long and short as well as using the hands to throw or roll the ball.

>> **1 v 1s:** Stopping and blocking attackers running at the goalkeeper.

The Loneliness of Goalkeeping

Goalkeeping is such a unique position in soccer that many books have been written just about the mental challenges of being a part of, but separate from, the rest of the team. There's even a famous soccer novel called *Goalkeepers Are Different* by the well-known British soccer journalist Brian Glanville.

So what makes goalkeeping different and what should you, the parent, keep in mind about the mental challenges?

REMEMBER

Perhaps the biggest challenge comes from the amount of pressure a goalkeeper feels and the scrutiny they receive from making a mistake. An error from a goalkeeper can often lead directly to a goal being scored. This may come from dropping the ball or failing to stop a soft shot. Most of the time, mistakes from outfield players don't lead so directly to goals for the other team. If a forward misplays a pass, it's not usually magnified in the same way.

TIP

Goals scored on a goalkeeper are far from always the goalkeeper's fault! Because they are usually the closest player to the ball when it goes in, it can sometimes feel (especially to the goalkeeper) that every goal is somehow their fault. But most goals are the result of a sequence of plays, often including mistakes from outfield players, that aren't immediately obvious. Soccer is a team game and it's key that if your child is a goalie, they realize that they can't save everything and goals going in is just part of the game.

This particular pressure and focus on the goalkeeping role makes mental resilience and toughness particularly important for goalkeepers. The natural reaction for most people to a mistake is to be frustrated, and it can feel like they have let the team down. Being able to work through the moment, shake off a mistake, and stay focused on the task at hand — goalkeeping — is a real challenge, but it is important mentally for a goalkeeper.

REMEMBER

Even the greatest goalkeepers in the history of soccer have made mistakes leading to goals, most of them many times over. Remind your child that it's not realistic for anyone to be perfect, even the best of the best.

Because of the separation of skills needed, the role of the goal-keeper, and even the uniform they wear, goalkeepers can often feel slightly distinct from the rest of the team. They are even often training away from their teammates, receiving specialized instruction. This is why goalkeepers can sometimes feel less integrated into the group.

TIP

It's important to remind your child that the rest of the team likely deeply appreciates all the efforts of the goalkeeper and sees them as a crucial part of the team. Bonding outside of prac-tices and games, such as the team going out for lunch together following a match, is a great way for the goalkeeper to get just as close to their teammates as anyone else.

3

Progressing at Home and Beyond

IN THIS CHAPTER

» **Improving at home with easy practice drills**

» **Taking advantage of technology**

» **Utilizing videos**

» **Securing private practice sessions**

» **Exploring the value of playing other sports**

Chapter **9**

Getting Better Outside Team Practice

I f your kid wants to improve their skills rapidly, one of the best ways to do this is to help them get some extra time on the ball and improve their understanding of the game outside of formal club soccer training.

If you're not an experienced soccer player yourself, it can be intimidating to try to work out how to help your child train effectively outside the usual structure of coaches leading them at practice.

Fortunately, there are very simple ways to get good touches on the ball at home as well as more advanced technology-driven methods and additional training programs to look into.

Practicing Simple Drills

Sometimes getting better at soccer is perceived to be more complicated and expensive than it needs to be. While this chapter explores many things that do cost more money — from training apps to private coaching — there are also a lot of simple ways to improve at home or at the nearest park with just a couple of relatively low-cost drills.

Rebounding the ball

Perhaps the most effective solo drill of all to get better at the game requires just two things — a soccer ball and a wall, or other hard surface to rebound the ball off. Some of the best players in the world spent hours every week repeatedly kicking the ball against a wall. It may sound repetitive, but spending just 20 minutes doing this a few times a week can get your kid thousands of touches improving ball control and a variety of kicking techniques as the ball comes back to them from different angles.

TIP

Any kind of wall can work for this, even a low retaining wall. You want to be sure the noise isn't annoying the neighbors, however!

If you don't have a wall at home or nearby, *soccer rebounders* can be purchased if you have a space in your yard or driveway — any grass space with around 10-x-20 feet of space will work for various sizes of rebounders. Soccer rebounders are rigid frames with tight polyethylene netting that springs the ball back to the player. The frames stand up themselves on any flat surface and are staked into the ground, so they can be placed anywhere with the appropriate space to kick the ball.

Rebounders come in a variety of shapes and sizes. For younger kids under the age of 7, anything under 6-x-4 feet is a large enough size for them to get plenty of target and rebound practice and can be purchased for $75 to $100. As kids get older and kicks become stronger, a larger rebounder can be helpful. A basic 12-x-6-foot rebounder can be found for $100 to $150.

Simply getting your kid out there kicking the ball against a wall or rebounder will improve their ball control and kicking ability from sheer repetition and the variety of angles the ball will come back to them. However, you can also add some intentional variations to help them develop specific techniques:

>> **Distance from wall/rebounder:** The player can vary their distance from the wall, which will develop different reaction times and speeds of the ball coming back to them. You can have your child do 2–3 minutes each at 2 yards, 5 yards, or 10 yards from the wall.

>> **One touch:** The player uses just one touch (kick) to return the ball to the wall. This can be done at different speeds and with different parts of the foot, focusing on the inside or outside in rotations.

>> **Multi-touch:** The player practices receiving the ball with one touch and then striking it back to the rebounder, rotating between two- and three-touch limits.

>> **Target practice:** As well as receiving and passing the ball back, harder strikes can be practiced that mimic shooting the ball. Some rebounders have target areas marked on them. If you have a wall, you can use painter's tape or chalk to mark out small areas to target shots at.

Juggling

Look up "soccer juggling skills" on YouTube and you'll find some incredible feats by players who can keep the ball in the air with just their feet or other parts of their body (except their hands, of course) hundreds or even thousands of times in a row. This can look impossible for anyone to master — and indeed, getting good enough to be a YouTube juggling star may take years. Don't let that scare your kid from learning to juggle the soccer ball: In fact, the skills honed by learning to juggle the ball in the air have strong benefits when they get to just 10 or 20 "juggles."

REMEMBER

A *juggle* is counted per touch of the ball, keeping it up in the air without it touching the ground. For example, a player may kick it in the air with the left foot, then head the ball, then kick it twice in a row with their right foot. That would count as four juggles. Once the ball touches the ground, the count starts over again.

Based on watching those YouTube videos, you may think juggling is a little bit of a showboating exercise — sort of like basketball players spinning balls on their fingers. It may look flashy and fun, but does it really serve any purpose for becoming a better soccer player? In the case of juggling, the answer is actually "yes." While just becoming a good juggler can't make you a good soccer player, the saying goes that every good soccer player is a good juggler. That's despite the fact that you will very, very rarely see anyone actually juggle the ball during a real soccer game or even training. However, the core skills needed to juggle the ball translate to actual skills needed on the soccer field. These skills include balance, coordination, and the ability to control the ball effectively.

TIP

It's not necessary for any player to be able to juggle the ball thousands of times and do the types of elaborate skills a YouTube soccer juggler does; a point of diminishing returns certainly kicks in. But if your young player can get comfortable enough to juggle the ball 50–100 times, they'll benefit enormously in comfort and skill with the ball.

So how can you help your kid develop good juggling skills? You can help with a few tips. You can even consider incentivizing practice at home with the ball. Summer holidays are a great time to encourage your child to juggle in the front yard, back yard, or nearest safe space. You can challenge them to hit a certain target number — 20, 50, or 100 — in return for a special privilege or monetary reward.

In terms of how you can help them technically, here are a couple of suggestions to share to soften the learning curve: It's not easy to keep a soccer ball up in the air multiple times. Beginner jugglers should start by holding the ball with both hands and dropping it onto their foot, kicking it with the laces and following these tips:

>> **Let the ball hit the ground:** This may seem counterintuitive, but like learning to ride a bike with stabilizers on first, it's not realistic for many players to simply be able to juggle the ball in the air right off the bat. Instead, a good way to hone skills is to kick the ball once in the air, let it hit the ground, and then grab the ball with both hands. This can

be repeated 10–20 times, alternating kicking the ball with the left and right foot.

>> **Kick and catch:** A similar concept, but this time your player will drop the ball and kick it up to their hands and catch it. This helps develop striking the ball in the center and being able to control where it goes. The key to juggling is keeping the ball close to you rather than chasing high kicks all over the yard. Repeat this until the player can get two to three kicks without catching it and then progress to adding more juggles.

REMEMBER

Ultimately, it takes practice, practice, practice to get good at juggling. Getting to the first 10 or 20 will really help your player's core soccer skills, so a focus on achieving that first is key. Once the player is over 20 juggles, it quickly becomes a fun challenge to keep improving!

Honing skills with cones

During the COVID-19 pandemic, one of the most popular replacements for soccer training when kids couldn't get together were drills with cones laid out on the ground. The player weaves between cones, mimicking the turns and movement required to dribble past opponents in real games. Although of course kids are playing together again after the pandemic, cone drills still have a place as supplemental training to refine skills.

To get started, purchase a set of disc cones at your local sporting goods store or online. A set of 25 discs can be bought for under $20. You'll need enough grass space to set out the cones, around 20-x-20 feet will work well.

The simplest drill is to set out 10 to 15 cones in a straight line, spacing each cone a couple of feet apart. Starting with the ball at their feet at the first cone, the player weaves in and out of the cones to the end and back again to the starting point.

Encourage your child to keep the ball as close as possible to their feet. This close control technique will make it harder for defenders to intercept the ball from them in real games.

The emphasis at first should be on controlling the ball well through the cones, rather than focusing on speed. As technique improves, challenges to go faster can be added.

Variations of technique kicking the ball can further train various important technical skills:

>> **Using one foot only:** Alternating between using just the right or left foot

>> **Outside of the foot:** Using just the outside of one or both feet to dribble through the cones

>> **Inside of the foot:** Using just the inside of the feet

>> **Undersoles:** Using the bottom of the shoe (under the toe) to dribble

These drills can be repeated several times and rotated for variation to keep it interesting.

Training the Tech-Driven Way

Can using technology help your child be a better soccer player? Is the future of soccer training and practice incorporating more and more technological elements, versus the old-fashioned methods of scrimmages or kicking the ball against the wall?

Tech-driven soccer centers

Over the past few years, many tech-driven indoor training centers have opened around the country, focused on soccer from a forward-thinking perspective. These centers promise that various tech-enhanced training methods can get your kid better, faster and have fun doing so.

All of that comes at an additional cost on top of what you may be paying for regular training and soccer camps, so if you do invest in taking your child to one of these centers, be sure that it's for the right reason: They want to get better and are happy and able to take on the additional training.

The premise of tech-driven soccer centers is that by doing more repetitions with the soccer ball and using technology to challenge players on their accuracy, track their performance, and focus on areas that need improvement, technical skills can be mastered faster.

The tech aspect comes in through multiple ways, but a few key skills and technology-centered drills focus on areas such as

>> **Honing accuracy:** Players need to hit targets with the ball. The targets have sensors that light up when hit accurately, counting a score during a certain period of timed play. Players are challenged to beat their best scores, with leaderboards counting the best scores across players at the center.

>> **Shooting practice:** Automatic feeders fire balls to the player who then shoots at a goal or target. This can provide many more opportunities to practice shooting in a shorter period of time than traditional methods that require a lot of time spent chasing and retrieving balls.

>> **Ball control:** The repetition from these types of drills can help players have ten times more touches on the ball in an hour-long session than in a game or regular training session. This can help improve control of the ball and the quality of a player's first touch receiving the ball.

Many centers offer the opportunity to book individual sessions focused on tech-driven drills. These can be paid for per session, though many centers also offer monthly memberships for better value for frequent visits. Individual sessions with a coach are often also available along with group or team training opportunities.

TIP

The widespread use of technology in youth soccer training is relatively new, so it can be difficult to evaluate and assess the effectiveness of the various drills and programs. However, if your child enjoys it and is getting more time actively playing with a soccer ball, it's surely only a good thing for their health and development.

The largest chain of tech-enhanced soccer training centers is Toca Soccer, an official partner of Major League Soccer. Toca

Soccer has more than 30 centers across the country; visit www.tocafootball.com to see if one is near you. In addition, there are many independent operators in various cities. Enter "tech-driven soccer" in your browser to see if you can locate one in your area.

Apps for home training

There's an app for everything these days — from timing your coffee brew to crossword puzzles. So it's no surprise that the app stores for Apple and Android devices are packed full of offerings that promise to rapidly improve your youth player's soccer skills.

Are they effective? Before I answer that, let's be clear that an app can only help in supplementary ways to become a better player. Playing soccer with other kids is the best way to improve, whether that's in team practice, games, or casual pickup play. Nothing can replicate the reality of how players move and understanding the game as it is played.

That said, like hitting the ball against a wall or practicing juggling, if the app encourages your child to get out there and get touches on the ball, it can encourage both healthy outdoor play and help develop ball skills.

So how do the apps work? At the heart of it, most soccer training apps provide a wide selection of drills that can be performed at home — in the yard or even in the living room — with players recording their completion of the task.

TIP

The benefit of the app is that it can show and explain to your player how to do the drill in a clear, structured way. Most training apps have a video showing step-by-step how to perform the task along with a description in text. Players can then track their time spent on the drill.

Some apps create training plans, essentially a series of varied drills the player needs to perform in sequence. These may be technically based around mastery of the ball or fitness-focused, depending on what the player selects. As in many types of apps, users are often "rewarded" with virtual prizes and can track their progress in leaderboards. Some apps even allow users to register with their club and compare performance against other players in their club. A few popular apps are

>> **Techne Futbol:** One of the most downloaded training apps, Techne has hundreds of drills organized into various sessions that focus on areas such as fundamental technical skills, dribbling, shooting, and physical training. Subscriptions start at $10 a month, though a free trial is available to check it out and see whether your player likes it. Techne offers the ability to navigate the app as either a parent or a youth player — unlike many apps that are focused on the player only.

>> **Train Effective Soccer App:** While it may not have the catchiest name, this app has a deep set of training drills, plans, and fitness exercises to work through. It also offers courses that dive deeper into tactics and the mental approach to the game, while the premium option includes the opportunity to speak directly with professional coaches, something more advanced players may enjoy. Various levels of monthly subscription are available.

>> **DribbleUp:** Unlike the apps I mention earlier, DribbleUp requires an additional prop to be purchased separately — a "smart" soccer ball. The ball pairs with the DribbleUp app so that the performance of drills can be tracked and recorded. The app features a series of drills that are focused on mastering the ball in tight spaces, allowing it to be used indoors or outside. DribbleUp is a more expensive option than some other training apps, requiring purchase of the ball as well as a monthly subscription.

Advancing via Video

You're reading a book about how your kid can play youth soccer and advance in the game, but it probably won't come as a surprise to you that there are lots of ways to utilize video technology to help in a way the printed word can't. That can include watching and learning from videos as well as, for more advanced players, even recording and analyzing your own child's play.

As with many things on the internet, searching for "youth soccer videos" will lead you quickly down rabbit holes of endless content that's difficult to filter through. It's important to start by thinking through what type of content will be useful to you and your young player: Are you looking for basic drills to do at home to get started or elite-level advice and insight?

The following sections provide a few categories to explore and suggested resources to look at.

Basic drills and skills

Nothing makes it easier to give your kids technical advice and examples they can follow than video, with breakdowns that zoom in on how to develop core skills quickly.

>> **Soccerdrive.com:** This website has a series of videos on the fundamentals of soccer. Presented without fluff or filler, these videos are a very simple guide to get quickly to the techniques of the basics of soccer such as heading, long passes, or accurate shooting.

>> **7mlc (on YouTube):** A U.S.-based professional soccer player from England, Michael Cunningham, focuses on skill drill videos that are easy to follow and range from developing fundamental techniques to challenges for the more advanced player.

>> **Progressive Soccer Training:** One of the longer-running training series, Progressive Soccer — run by Dylan Tooby — has hundreds of short drills clearly explained without extra fuss or fluff. The series includes videos specifically designed for parents of youth soccer players to help introduce basic drills to their kids.

>> **Unisport:** A YouTube channel with five million subscribers, Unisport initially focused on reviewing soccer cleats. But they've also developed a strong following for their soccer technique–focused videos, with a series of tutorials focused on skills such as curving the ball or improving speed.

Advice for advanced players

When your kid is ready to look at next-level techniques, perhaps looking to play elite soccer and even aspiring to play college or professional soccer, there are a number of YouTube channels that focus on gaining an edge. This can include detailed technical skill move drills, tips from pro players on how they handle match situations, and advice on getting recruited for college programs. A few channels worth checking out include

>> **Become Elite:** YouTuber Matt Sheldon (@BecomeElite), a professional soccer player in the United States, offers a lot of clear and accessible advice on everything from how to write recruiting emails to college coaches to breaking down what advanced skills actually matter to hit the next level. Sheldon's down-to-earth videos are insightful and easy to watch, and they also show life behind the scenes as a hard-working professional player.

>> **Beast Mode Soccer:** Want to see some drills many top players run through? Beast Mode Soccer has worked with many leading professionals, including multiple U.S. Women's National Team players, providing excellent examples of the best running through practice challenges.

>> **All Attack (www.youtube.com/allattack):** While some YouTube channels focus on the personalities of the presenters to make their points, the All Attack channel offers super slo-mo breakdowns of skill moves to show techniques in clear and minute detail. Examples from real-life professional games of the same skills or moves are added to bring the techniques to life.

Freestyle fun and games

Want to have your mind blown on what some women and men can do with a soccer ball? Some players have mastered control of the ball to the point where it feels like they have it on a string, controlling a large sphere with their feet with more ease than most of us can handle a ball with our hands. The content on these types of channels is light fare, but it can inspire your kid to try some new tricks and spend more time with the ball:

>> Séan Garnier (@seanfreestyle on YouTube), a former professional player and long-time freestyler, entertains viewers with freestyle juggling challenges recorded with

top current and former professional soccer players and even athletes from other sports, such as the NBA. Beyond the glitzy matchups and contests, though, you can also find playlists of freestyle tutorials with tips on how to try to perform some of the ridiculous skills on display.

>> The YouTube channel @YourHowToDo is led by professional Irish freestyler Dara Coyne. The channel features interviews with top freestylers and clips from freestyle "battles" between professionals showcasing their tricks. There's also an extensive library of step-by-step tutorials for a variety of moves, flicks, and skills that are presented in a clear, no-nonsense style.

>> Street Socccer International (@StreetSoccerInt) on YouTube releases fresh episodes each week covering street soccer and freestyle moves. There's quite a bit of light and somewhat silly content — "MAN vs dog" contesting soccer skills, anyone? — but also plenty of skill move guides and highlights from global street soccer events to inspire your youngster.

One-on-One Training

If you and your child are looking to get some extra training in outside team practice, a popular option is to sign up for private soccer lessons with one coach training your player. The advantage of one-on-one coaching sessions is the total focus on your player's development. It provides a supplementary focus that can drill into an individual's soccer skills and areas they may need to improve upon. Because there's only one player, your kid gets a lot of touches on the ball and the chance for continual, immediate feedback from a coach dedicated during that time to that player.

WARNING

Private training sessions usually last one hour at a time. If your child also has soccer practice and games several other times a week, private training should only be added once or twice a week. Otherwise, you risk burning out your kid on too much soccer.

What to look for in a trainer

Private soccer lessons are a bit of a Wild West, as anyone can set themselves up as a trainer without needing specific certification. Using a reputable training service can help, as you can feel relatively confident the trainer has undergone some vetting to show their credentials and has some experience with other players.

Here are some questions to ask:

>> **What is the trainer's experience with playing and coaching soccer?** While elite players (who have played professionally or in high-level college soccer) don't always translate into the best trainers, it's important that they have good proven experience either as a top player or with multiple years as a coach in a recognized youth soccer club or academy. While you can't rule out the possibility that someone without either experience may make a good coach, it's hard to trust that they'll have the necessary experience.

>> **What age and level of players does the trainer usually work with?** There's no point hiring someone who specializes in high school kids preparing for college showcase events for your 10-year-old just starting out with soccer. You'll probably overpay on their rate, and they may not be attuned to working with younger children needing more basic development. Find someone with experience at the right age and competitive level.

>> **What's their track record?** Ask who they have worked with. If you can find someone another parent you know has hired and recommends, that's a great starting point. Otherwise, ask for recommendations. Be wary of reviews on websites or social media, which may or may not be genuine and representative.

TIP

Many trainers or training services have prominent social media presences. They may show lots of great videos that look like a great proof of concept. But remember: These social media accounts are carefully curated, and a lot of the content can be staged. This type of content is understandable — just be sure that you aren't taking everything you see at face value.

How to find a trainer

Prominent nationwide services include Dribbler (dribbler soccer.com) and Coach Up (www.coachup.com). Local youth soccer clubs or facilities may also offer private training. Check websites of the ones local to you or give them a call to find out.

TIP

Your player's youth soccer coach may also offer private lessons, even if they don't advertise that they do. If the coach has a good rapport with your child, ask if they'd consider offering private sessions. The bonus here is that you already know the coach and additional sessions can potentially be arranged conveniently before or after team training sessions.

Individual training fees

Costs vary around the country for individual trainers, but expect on average to pay $60 to $70 per hour. This cost can be reduced per hour with some trainers or training services if you sign up and commit to multiple sessions or months of training.

Highly experienced coaches for players at the elite level approaching college or professional level may charge over $100 per hour.

TIP

Many coaches also offer small group training (two to four players), which can be a more affordable option with some of the hourly training cost split among multiple players.

Playing Other Sports

In decades past, many of the best athletes in America played — and excelled — at multiple sports. Think of Bo Jackson, an all-star in two sports (baseball and American football), or Deion Sanders (same sports as Bo). Or Bob Hayes, a 100-meter champion in the Olympics and an NFL Hall of Famer.

Nowadays, professional athletes who play more than one sport are rarer and that seems to be increasingly true in youth soccer. But if your kid does want to compete or even just have fun in different sports, there are a lot of good reasons to encourage this, including

>> **Broad athletic development:** Playing multiple sports can develop different muscles, contribute to strength and flexibility development, and aid overall fitness in a more balanced way.

>> **Avoiding burnout:** The opportunity to have fun playing another sport can balance out your child's activities.

>> **Injury prevention:** Specialization in one sport can put a lot of stress on the body. Broader athletic development can help strengthen the body holistically, which can help prevent injuries.

TIP

The simplest way to keep your child playing multiple sports is to add an individual sport on top of a team sport. Individual play can be scheduled more flexibly since they are less dependent on the rigid planning required for team training with many participants. Some sports are particularly complimentary to soccer in terms of the movement and flexibility they help develop, which can translate well to the soccer field. For example, gymnastics and karate both help develop flexibility and agility, while the quick movements in tennis translate well to the quick turns needed in soccer. However, it's more important simply to get a variety of exercise in whichever other sports your child enjoys the most.

Chapter **10**

Playing Futsal and Pickup Soccer

P laying different variants of soccer with other kids outside organized soccer practice is a great way for your young player to have more fun and develop their skills. This type of casual soccer — which builds friendships outside of soccer and is a productive way to spend hours of time off a phone screen and doing something active — hasn't traditionally been massively popular in America. But that's starting to change. Read on to find out how your kid can get more soccer in their life.

Picking Up Some Extra Soccer

In London, England, they play at the parks or on the concrete on small-sided fields. In Brazil, the beaches are a soccer playground, and in Africa, kids are playing nonstop with makeshift goals anywhere there is enough space to play, whatever the surface. In America, unfortunately, we do not have quite the same culture of kids playing soccer outside in the parks and streets. The increasing trend for children to spend more time on screens rather than being outside hardly helps in this regard — a challenge not unique to soccer, of course.

So, unfortunately, getting your kid playing some extra soccer isn't as easy as opening the front door and sending them out onto the streets in most places. But don't despair; there are some easy ways to get your kid playing some casual soccer.

REMEMBER

What are the benefits of getting some extra soccer in your kid's life?

>> Playing more outside — whether soccer or other activities — is shown to help with the physical and mental well-being of children.

>> Casual soccer is usually low cost. If your child is playing club soccer, you're already likely spending a lot of money, so this can be a great way to add more play without extra cost.

>> Pickup sports where children are running the show (rather than following structured adult organization in practices) generates good problem- and conflict-solving skills, leadership, and teamwork.

>> It can be a great opportunity for your kid to build friendships without a lot of adult involvement or intervention.

>> The low-pressure setting can encourage kids to try new skills and be creative in play.

Unless you're lucky enough to live in an area where you see kids gathering to play already in parks or other locations, some casual and pickup soccer may take a little proactive work by you and other parents to get going.

If you have a yard big enough for a couple of small pop-up goals, it can be as easy as inviting a few of your child's friends over and having them kick the ball around. Set this up and you may find that from there, your kid will be out there playing and having friends join in without much involvement from you (depending on their age, of course).

Another option is to set up some soccer playtime at the local park with other parents bringing their kids out. The beauty of soccer is that all you need to do is set up a couple of goals — if you don't have pop-up goals, even cones will do for posts. Throw a ball out there and let them run!

Finally, there are "organized" pickup sessions available via some youth soccer clubs or at soccer training centers. Search Google or check with soccer club and center websites to see if they offer any open pickup sessions for kids in the right age group for you.

Understanding Futsal

You may see that your club is running "futsal" programs, camps, or leagues and wonder, What on earth is futsal and why should my child play?

The technical answer is that *futsal* is a scaled-down, five-a-side version of soccer usually played indoors. It features a special smaller ball that is heavier and bounces less than a regular ball. Futsal is always played on a hard surface rather than on grass.

The more important answer is that futsal can provide a whole new style of playing soccer for your kid that can rapidly improve their foot skills and provide a lot of fast and furious fun, so it's definitely worth exploring.

Finding out more about futsal

TECHNICAL STUFF

The word "futsal" comes from a shortening of the Spanish words "fútbol sala," which directly translated means "hall football" — referring to soccer being played indoors in a gymnasium hall or basketball court.

This form of soccer was pioneered in the 1930s in Uruguay, then one of the great soccer nations (winners of the inaugural 1930 World Cup). Playing in gyms on a basketball-sized court offered more places to play in all weather conditions. In addition, with just five players on each side, futsal requires fewer team members for a match than traditional 11-a-side games outdoors. This form of the game was quickly adopted, and players found it helped develop their skills well for outdoor play as well.

Futsal became popular across South America very rapidly and has long been credited with helping develop the excellent technical skills players from that continent are known for. Many top world stars, such as Lionel Messi and Neymar, grew up playing futsal and credit the game for helping them reach the top.

TIP

Because futsal is played on a smaller court than traditional soccer and has a smaller, heavier ball, players develop excellent ball control skills working in tight spaces. Players also get a lot more touches with one ball being played among 10 players versus 22 in full-size soccer.

The fast pace and need to be accurate controlling or passing the ball accelerates the development of fundamental soccer skills that then translate well to playing traditional outdoor soccer. Futsal is also good at letting players hone their ability to make quick decisions based on the fast-moving nature of the game. It translates well to larger traditional formats of soccer because players often have to take actions in a smaller space in futsal.

The futsal court

Futsal is relatively easy to set up because it can be played indoors or outdoors on a hard surface around the size of a basketball court. It's often played in gymnasiums that are also used for other sports like basketball or volleyball.

REMEMBER

Unlike a lot of traditional indoor soccer fields in the United States, futsal is played on a court without walls for the ball to bounce off. Like outdoor soccer, lines mark the out of bounds surrounding the field of play. This reduces the risk of injury, as players aren't banging into walls.

TIP

Playing without walls surrounding the field is considered a plus for futsal in developing skillful players, because without a wall, passes have to be accurate in the small space of a futsal court or the ball will go out of play. Playing with walls is more forgiving since the ball always stays in play bouncing away.

The goal at either end of a futsal court differs in size from traditional outdoor goals, coming in smaller. It measures 10' wide by 6'5" high.

The futsal ball

One of the most obvious and impactful differences between futsal and soccer is the ball itself. The futsal ball is smaller than a regular soccer ball and is slightly heavier, resulting in less bounce.

This is intentional — by utilizing a less bouncy ball, it's easier to play in smaller spaces without the ball flying off and bouncing out of bounds all the time. The smaller size and heavier weight make it easier to control the ball, which helps with the intricate play futsal encourages.

There are two primary sizes of futsal balls:

>> **Size 4:** Used for players 13 years and over and equivalent in size to a size 4 regular soccer ball (smaller than a regular size 5 ball players at this age would use)

>> **Size 3:** Used for younger players under the age of 13 and equivalent in size to a size 3 regular soccer ball

TIP

Futsal balls can easily be purchased online at soccer retailers or general sporting goods outlets (or Amazon). A good ball costs around $30.

Futsal rules

Most of the rules of traditional soccer apply to futsal (see Chapter 1 for a primer). Some things, though, are distinct to this form of the game:

>> Futsal teams feature fewer players than outdoor soccer. Each team has five players, with the goalkeeper counting as one of these players.

>> Futsal games are shorter. Adult games consist of 20-minute halves at the professional level versus 90 minutes for 11-a-side soccer. Youth games usually have 15-minute halves versus longer 25- or 30-minute halves outdoors in under-13 age groups.

>> There are no throw-ins in futsal. Play is restarted by the team kicking the ball in.

- » There are no goal kicks in futsal. Play is restarted by the goalkeeper rolling or throwing the ball into play.

- » There is no offside rule in futsal. Attacking players can stand anywhere on the court when receiving the ball.

- » The game does not need to be stopped for a substitution to take place. Players can replace each other on the fly (similar to ice hockey).

- » Teams are able to deploy one timeout per half to pause play.

- » A player receiving a red card is removed from the game, but after a two-minute sanction, that player can be replaced by a substitute.

Futsal positions and skills

Futsal has a lot more similarities than differences in how it is played compared to traditional soccer, but there are some nuances to the game that can be helpful to know.

Goalkeeping

The goalkeeper is one of the five players, and in futsal, is much more frequently involved in the play than in outdoor soccer. Because the field is smaller, futsal goalies face more frequent shots and often have to use their feet and legs more frequently to block the ball.

Goalkeepers are also more involved in setting up the play by either throwing or kicking the ball to launch attacks. Goalkeepers in futsal have even been compared to the role of quarterbacks in (American) football. They need to have very good foot skills to be successful.

Fixo

In front of the goalkeeper is typically the lone dedicated defender, known as the *fixo*, which is a Portuguese term for a player "fixed" in one place (in this case, defending the goal).

Don't take the term "fixed" too literally — the *fixo* must move around following the run of play and can also venture up to attack. But the term does sum up their main role of protecting the goalkeeper, trying to anticipate attacks and snuff them out. The *fixo* also plays an important role in orchestrating the team and passing the ball into attacking situations.

Wingers

Playing on the left- and right-hand sides of the court — its wings, hence the name *winger* — these players work hard getting up and down the court both defending and attacking. These are energetic positions for players with good stamina and all-around skills to both help stop attacks as well as make key passes and shoot on goal.

Pivot

The furthest forward player is typically known as the *pivot*, providing the focal point for the team in the attacking area of the court. The term *pivot* is used because play often revolves around this player, who frequently receives the ball and turns to make another move — whether a pass, shot, or dribble. Players in this position need to have the ability to control the ball and hold off defenders, dribble with the ball, and make strong shots on goal.

Getting on the futsal court

Futsal programs aren't nearly as ubiquitous around the country as regular soccer, but there are a growing number of places to play and helpful resources to get your kid on the court. Check with your child's club first to see whether they offer any programming.

Aside from traditional soccer clubs, there are now many dedicated futsal programs and even facilities in a growing number of cities. The US Youth Futsal website (www.usyouthfutsal.com) is a good starting point to find programs in your area, with a directory of affiliated clubs nationwide. Google searches for your city can also help uncover programs. You can also ask your child's soccer coach whether they know of any futsal programming locally.

Developing Skills in Small-Sided Soccer

Similar to the value of futsal, playing any kind of *small-sided soccer* — teams with between three and five players each — is loads of fun and provides a lot of touches on the ball. Lots of touches on the ball means that your kid is more involved in the run of play, likely leading to greater enjoyment and skill development.

Recreational and club soccer should already be played among small-sided teams until the age of 7. Outside of team play, look for other opportunities to get your child playing compact versions of the game. Even once your kids are over 10 and playing in competitive soccer programs, continuing to play smaller-sided soccer can help them get better and have more fun.

3-versus-3 tournaments

Three-versus-three soccer features three players on each team shooting on small goals on a small pitch without goalkeepers. This format is relatively common and often organized into tournament formats, particularly during the off season for club matches in the winter or summer.

Given the small number of players needed on each team, it can be pretty easy to put together a group from your child's teammates or other friends they play soccer with. That can make playing a really fun experience.

TIP

The main benefit of 3-versus-3 is due to the low number of players. Everyone on the pitch gets plenty of touches on the ball and gets to play a variety of positions, both defending and attacking. This can give your child great experience in areas of the field they might not focus on during larger matches on bigger fields with more specialized positions.

5- or 6-a-side

The other most common small-sided format features five or six players on each team. In this case, goalkeepers are on the field, so there are four or five players in outfield positions.

We've already explored futsal, which is a specific 5-a-side format. But you'll also see other games of 5-a-side played indoors and outdoors. Six-a-side soccer is the traditional format used in indoor soccer played with walls (similar to an ice rink). This version of the game used to be very popular, though it is now considered to be less helpful in developing skills than futsal or other formats that play without walls.

Regardless of the exact format, every small-sided format game typically provides plenty of fun and is a positive way to enhance skill development outside of traditional club soccer matches and practice sessions.

TIP

Small-sided games are helpful for players to further develop because they mirror the regular game format but provide more involvement in the game. Compared to games with more players and larger fields, players get more touches and need to make faster decisions with the ball. This type of play prepares the player well for the bigger format game and, just as importantly, is a lot of fun.

Chapter **11**

Specialized Training Camps

Developmental soccer camps offer opportunities for immersion into soccer for several days or even weeks at a time. These are different from recreational soccer camps, where the emphasis is on fun and enjoyment.

These camps are suited for competitive players looking to develop skills in preparation for the upcoming club season or to accelerate development during the year.

Your current club may offer camps, but you aren't tied to going with them — an array of options is out there from different organizers that focus on all kinds of areas of the game, which I explore in this chapter.

The Benefits of Going to Camp

Camps are a great way to get your kid to play plenty of soccer, improve fitness, and make new friends. Because there are no games to keep score around, coaches can focus fully on developmental skill progression for players over short but intensive periods of time. Players thus reap quick benefits, especially in technical or tactical elements of the game.

REMEMBER

Camps do add another expensive investment on top of other fees you may already be paying for participation in soccer programs. Fees range widely depending on the type of camp being offered and especially how many hours and days it runs. It's important, then, to have a good understanding of all the benefits in going to soccer camp and weigh up which option — if any — is right for your child.

Like many types of camp, soccer camps get your kid out of the house during the summer and other school holidays for productive, outdoor exercise. With kids spending more and more time on screens and indoors, the intentional structure of soccer camps taking your child onto the field and off a device is in itself a big win, along with having them be more physically active.

Camps also put a lot of kids together over an extended period of time, which is likely to help your young soccer player develop friendships and social skills through bonding on and off the field. They also put children on their own in a different, unfamiliar environment away from home or school, which can be an important step in developing independence and self-reliance.

Kids also usually get a fun takeaway or two from the camp — a t-shirt, uniform, and if the camp is run by a local professional soccer club, sometimes also tickets to a match.

TIP

From a soccer perspective, camps can also help accelerate skill development; enhance fitness through hours of play each day; and at advanced levels, provide specialized training to work on areas of weakness.

Summer camps also provide a bridge to continue playing soccer in what is usually a break in club play, allowing for development and potentially bonding with current or future teammates.

Selecting a Camp

In any large metropolitan area, and even in smaller cities or towns, you can find plenty of camp options to consider for your child. These camps are run by a variety of organizations, from local soccer clubs to some of the best-known soccer teams in the world.

Local youth club camps

Camps are a big part of any local youth soccer club's business. Professional soccer clubs in various American leagues also offer camps that are often connected to their own youth soccer programming.

Check the websites of clubs in your area to see what they have available. If your kid is already on a competitive club program, the easiest option is to sign up for a camp offered by your club.

Clubs generally encourage players to take part in their own camps for obvious reasons: It provides the core of their customers for the camp and also offers a continuity in coaching for their players.

TIP

Camps can also be a way to experience the coaching environment and facilities of another club. If you're considering switching clubs at some point, this can be a helpful way to find out more about other options and get to know some of the coaches and administrators.

College-based camps

College soccer programs often run soccer camps utilizing their facilities and deploying their varsity team players to serve as instructors.

These camps can serve two purposes depending on the age group being served:

>> **Traditional youth soccer camps:** These camps, especially for younger age groups, have the same focus and programming described throughout this chapter.

>> **ID camps:** For older kids, some camps run by colleges are promoted as *ID camps* to give college coaches the opportunity to scout potential future recruits. These camps give players the chance to show their skills in front of coaches from the college hosting and sometimes additional visiting coaches from other colleges.

These camps are aimed at high school athletes who play competitively and hope to play in college. Sometimes the programming is designed to replicate aspects of the college soccer training experience.

TIP

Attending a college ID camp doesn't necessarily mean your young player is getting a massive leg up on the recruiting competition, but it certainly doesn't hurt. At the least, this type of camp is likely to be a good experience and development opportunity, as ID camps are typically well run.

International club–run camps

Many famous professional teams from other countries offer camps under their iconic branding in the United States. These can sound fantastic — after all, they are world-famous clubs — and they are usually very well marketed.

TIP

However, don't expect these camps to feature actual coaches from the likes of Real Madrid or Paris Saint Germain. These programs usually recruit local coaches and follow a curriculum provided by the parent club's youth programming division.

The actual experience of training at these camps is usually very similar to other local club camps but with the added glitz of being surrounded by a world-famous club's brand. Players will likely receive a branded uniform and other goodies included in the cost of attending.

If your child is a fan of that club, they'll certainly love the opportunity to train in team gear and feel like they are a part of the club. If that excitement is genuine for your child, then these camps can be a great experience.

REMEMBER

Because of the prestigious global brands these camps are trading on, fees can be considerably higher than for local youth soccer club camps. The quality of the coaching and training is similar, so just remember that you are essentially paying for that brand experience rather than anything likely to significantly advance their soccer development or get them a shot to play for a world-famous team.

Residential overnight camps

Does your kid want to literally eat, breathe, and sleep soccer? Overnight camps during the summer vacation period offer immersion over multi-day periods in which your kid will experience soccer all day and evening.

These residential sessions allow for an expansive array of training covering technical skills, tactical and mental approach insights in the classroom, physical work in the gym, and games.

Camps like these are often hosted by colleges using dormitory facilities but can have various organizers, from MLS clubs to colleges.

A typical residential schedule may look like this:

>> 7 a.m: Wake-up call

>> 7:30 a.m: Breakfast

>> 8:30 a.m–10:00 a.m: Field session

>> 10:00 a.m–11:30 a.m: Classroom session

>> 11:30 a.m–12:30 p.m: Lunch break

>> 12:30 p.m–2 p.m: Field session

>> 4 p.m–5 p.m: Recovery session

>> 5 p.m–6 p.m: Dinner

>> Evening: Scrimmages and small-sided soccer

>> 10 p.m: Lights out

Residential camps are for very motivated players and those comfortable being away from family for a few days. These offerings typically start at the U8 age level and go up to U18.

TIP

If you live close to the camp location, sometimes it's possible to attend the camp as a "commuter" coming in for the camp each day. This may be a good option if your child isn't yet comfortable sleeping away from home for multiple days.

Decoding Camp Schedules and Fees

All of these camp options and the variety of organizing bodies inevitably means that there's quite a bit of variance in the cost. But they generally follow a formula of availability and come within a range of costs for you to consider.

Camp calendars and schedules

Soccer camps are typically offered most frequently when school is out, so this, of course, varies by local area. Summer holidays, being the longest, can provide multiple weeks of options across various local camps.

Depending how motivated your child is to play and how much you can invest in camps to build your child's soccer skills (and potentially help with childcare needs), you may even place your player in more than one camp during the summer.

Camps also are often held during other school breaks, especially in the winter. Depending on your region's climate, these will more likely than not have an indoor setting.

TIP

One-off single day camps are also often offered around other holidays such as Thanksgiving or Martin Luther King Jr. Day.

Camp dates can be found on the websites of clubs and organizations offering them, usually around six months before they take place.

Some camps, especially in the summer, have great reputations and book up fast given that limited spots are available. So be sure to plan camps well in advance and secure a spot early.

Camp timings

Day camps generally fall into two categories for their hours of operation, half day or full day. Both typically start at 9 a.m, though this can vary by an hour on either side, with a check-in period for campers arriving on their first day.

Some camps may allow you to drop off your kid an hour early if that's helpful for your schedule. This usually comes at an additional cost.

After check-in, camps jump into their programming of drills until lunchtime, probably with a snack break halfway through the morning.

At lunchtime, around noon, half-day campers depart the camp.

Full-day campers jump back into more programming after lunch. That may include focused drills followed by scrimmages to end the day with pickup often set for 3 p.m.

The cost of attending camp

Specialized soccer camps range in fees depending on the type of camp and the organization running them, but you can typically expect the following:

>> Half-day camp (four or five days): $150–$250

>> Full-day camp (four or five days): $400–$600

>> Day camp (single day): $75–$125

>> Residential camp (weeklong overnight): $700–$1,000

If the camp is at the upper end of these fee ranges, ask what justifies the higher cost. Perhaps it's a low player-to-coach ratio, outstanding facilities, or specialized coaches coming in for the camp. Don't be afraid to ask the program what makes their camp special and justifies their fees.

Types of Technical Camps

One of the great advantages of specialized training camps is they can allow a singular focus on one particular area of play or positioning over many hours of play, which isn't typically possible in regular team practice.

This type of specialization may characterize an entire camp program, or a multi-day camp may be segmented into chunks that focus on various specific areas.

Camps can allow a focus on one area of the game that can rapidly enhance a player's skills that may otherwise take weeks to develop in regular team training programming.

Ask your player's coach if they have a recommendation for an area of play your child may want to focus on to advance their skills. This may reinforce a skill set relevant to their position — for example, shooting for a striker — or it may be helpful for them to work on areas that they haven't spent as much time developing.

Defending the goal

Developmental camps for defenders hone in on the art of defensive play to be able to both cut off attacks effectively and build an attack from the back of the field.

This may include a focus on skills such as

>> One-on-one defending

>> Tackling and challenging opponents

>> Positioning on the field

>> Intercepting and clearing the ball

>> Distribution and passing

Controlling the midfield

Involved heavily in both attacking and defending, midfielder position camps often focus on a mix of versatile skills. This helps players to advance their understanding and ability to possess the ball and move away from the ball to be effective in controlling the middle of the park.

Curriculums focused on this area likely include

>> Mastering the ball

>> Receiving the ball

>> Possessing the ball

>> Making decisions

Focusing on finishing

Ideal for attacking players, these camps — which may also be called "finishing camps" or "attacker camps" — cover areas to enhance sharp shooting and contributing to teamwork:

>> One-on-one finishing

>> Shooting from distance

>> Shooting from angles

>> Holding up the ball

>> Headers and volleys

TIP

Camps for both strikers and goalkeepers or strikers and defenders are also fairly common. Goalkeepers can provide the goalkeeping needed to practice stopping shots on goal and vice versa. And similarly, defenders and attackers can challenge each other.

Fitness, speed, and agility camps

Camps focused on developing physical attributes needed to succeed in soccer apply to players across all positions.

This type of camp can help players with their running mechanics, conditioning, movement, and ball skills, instilling and instructing them on areas that players can continue and bring into their ongoing training routine.

Goalkeeping camps

As I note a couple of times in this book, goalkeepers are different — utilizing unique skill sets. So naturally, there are dedicated camps for goalkeeping.

The focus of these camps is on goalkeeper–specific skills covering

>> Diving and shot stopping

>> Handling the ball

>> Distributing the ball

>> Playing one-on-one

>> Dealing with crosses into the box

Chapter **12**

Considering School Soccer

I n many American sports, playing for your school is the peak place to participate in that sport, with college scouts looking for top players, large crowds coming out on Friday nights, and even some games televised nationally. Think about how popular high school football is in Texas! Soccer, though, isn't quite as all-in on school play. Club soccer is generally prioritized by competitive players, who don't all participate in school play.

While the level of play in top high schools for soccer is certainly very strong, the season is short and not all the top players in each state take part — either out of choice to focus on club soccer, or because their club doesn't permit them to play additional school soccer.

Despite that, there's still a big place for school soccer as an option for many players to enjoy playing alongside friends and make memorable moments. I explain the school soccer ecosystem in detail in this chapter and help you understand how to discuss the option with your young player.

Understanding School Soccer's Place

From a purely competitive standpoint, there isn't much debate in most areas about whether the strongest teams are at high school or club soccer. The top club teams are able to select "all-star" players from across various schools and typically boast greater resources in terms of coaches and facilities than do local schools. Competing in the top levels of club soccer is more likely to provide a higher level of development and competition than school soccer ever can.

REMEMBER

However, the fact that school soccer isn't the highest level of play shouldn't deter you and your child from exploring the option of playing for their school, especially if they are not at the very tip-top of the competitive soccer pyramid — which of course most players aren't.

There is more to playing the sport than just looking for the ultimate competitive environment. As I stress throughout the book, it's important to enjoy soccer and the fun it brings on its own terms.

School soccer can provide kids the chance to play with friends (and make closer friendships) at their school and play for the pride of their school. School teams can be a community rallying point and build camaraderie among players and families. And many schools do provide further excellent training and development for their players with committed coaches.

TIP

School sports are also typically much less expensive than club sports. If the high fees of club soccer are challenging, school soccer can be a great option for your kid to play competitive soccer at a lower cost. As well as providing programming for lower registration fees than clubs, schools usually cover the cost of traveling to road games as the team all hops on a school bus together.

Juggling School and Club Soccer

If your child is playing competitive club soccer, or even recreational soccer with multiple practices and games a week, adding school soccer on top of that and any other activities they may do can feel daunting.

However, while club soccer is practically a year-round commitment, it's important to note that school soccer seasons are much shorter. Middle- and high-school seasons are typically 10–14 weeks long, taking place in the fall in most areas.

Practice begins just a couple of weeks before the first game takes place and is usually held twice per week after school in the afternoon or early evening.

Unlike club soccer, matches often take place on weekdays in the evening, though some weekend games are also scheduled, especially in high school play.

So while juggling of schedules is certainly required to make it work, school soccer only crosses over with club soccer for a short period of time. In some regions, club soccer seasons are also intentionally aligned to minimize crossover with school soccer, making it easier to participate in both.

There's no doubt, though, that playing both club and school soccer adds to an already heavy annual soccer participation calendar. If your child has interests in other activities as well, it may be very difficult to add school soccer to the schedule. Consider what may be best for a balanced approach.

TIP

Check with your middle or high school for the soccer season schedule and compare this to the club soccer season. If practice schedules conflict between school and club soccer, it'll be difficult to participate in both. Although some coaches may be understanding about your child missing some club or school practices, a lot of coaches expect their players to attend most practices.

REMEMBER

The season in which play takes place depends on what geographic region your state is in. Many warmer weather states play school soccer in the winter, while colder weather states compete early in the fall right after the school year begins.

Playing Middle-School Soccer

Going to middle school is a big leap from elementary school, and fitting in can be difficult to do. After-school activities are often a good way for any kid to bond with new friends and get excited about school-related activities.

From a social perspective, then, middle-school soccer can offer a great way for your kid to meet other girls or boys who enjoy soccer and make new friendships, which may last into high school as well.

TIP

The level and quality of play in middle-school soccer is unlikely to be incredibly high compared to that of club soccer teams or high-school soccer. The coaching drills, scrimmages, and games aren't likely to match those types of programs, so it's important not to go into middle-school soccer expecting your child to improve greatly on a technical level, especially with a relatively short season of play.

Remember that unlike the coaches in club soccer, middle school coaches are not likely to be dedicated soccer coaches and may have relatively little training or experience in the game. That may be made up for in enthusiasm for the sport or in building a great culture of enjoyment among the players, and such a positive atmosphere can often be the best part of middle-school soccer.

Balancing Club and High-School Soccer

Helping your child decide whether to play school soccer or not at the high school level is likely a difficult decision to be wrestled with if they are playing competitive soccer in a club program, and especially so if they are on an advanced-level team that is already providing an intense amount of soccer.

TIP

Check whether your state's high school athletic association has any specific rules that impact participation, as rules vary across the country. These rules can cover areas such as the number of sports a player can participate in and whether players can participate in both high school and club sports.

While the schedules I describe earlier in the chapter don't overlap year-round, there may be periods where your child is on both club and high-school soccer teams — or at the least, a bunch more soccer will be added to the calendar.

REMEMBER

If you're feeling like burnout is already a real risk given the volume of soccer your child is participating in on the club side, it's critical to give very careful thought to adding more time to playing the sport into a packed teenage schedule. Will your child be able to take on even more mental and physical demands with the extra practices and games?

On the flip side, playing school soccer has an upside to it that club soccer can't often match: the pride of representing your school community and playing alongside friends from school. Your child may already be missing a lot of bonding activities with friends due to the demands of playing travel soccer.

Ironically, playing more soccer alongside buddies from school can provide an opportunity to make memories on and off the field that may otherwise be missed due to their challenging club soccer schedule.

TIP

Playing on a school team may also provide them opportunities to develop as a player in a different way than on their club team. Your child may get to play in a different position and assume a leadership role that may not be the case on their club team.

Playing on the High-School Soccer Team

Getting onto the high-school team roster typically requires going to tryouts in advance of the season, usually held shortly after the start of the school year. You will probably need to register your child in advance for school athletics, which may incur a registration fee (probably under $100), and you may be asked to provide medical clearance as well.

Tryouts are often held on multiple days in 60- to 90-minute sessions after school.

Depending on the size of the school, the coach will likely be looking at a lot of players during the tryouts and there'll almost certainly be a very wide range of players with differing skill levels and understanding of the game.

TECHNICAL STUFF

High-school soccer games feature 11 versus 11 players. Schools typically have 16 to 18 players on a roster, allowing for a rotation of players who start and substitute in during games.

Many schools have multiple teams. The highest level is the "varsity" team, which features the players the coaches consider to be the most skilled and experienced available — often juniors or seniors.

There are often also teams below the varsity level, including "junior varsity" (JV) levels. These teams may have slightly lower practice frequency and intensity compared to the varsity team. They are often populated by younger high-school players in their sophomore or freshman years.

Team placements are made following the tryouts. It's possible your child won't make the cut onto any team; this is, of course, disappointing. How competitive a process this is depends entirely on the size of the school and the relative quality of players at the school.

Fortunately, if your kid misses the cut, there are many other options to play soccer at the recreational and club levels as outlined in earlier chapters.

Getting going with JV

If your young soccer player does make it onto a JV team, encourage them to embrace the opportunity even if perhaps they had hoped to make varsity. Remind them that they'll likely receive more playing time on the JV team and will be playing with and against those similar to their level of play.

Good performance on the JV team can often lead to opportunities in the future to play varsity, especially if they are a freshman or sophomore.

TIP

JV players may get the opportunity to play on a varsity team on a guest basis for a game or tournament. Spots often open up due to injuries or other reasons. Varsity players may be unavailable to take part, meaning rosters need to be filled. This can provide a good chance for your player to sample a higher level of play, get to know their coaches and teammates, and see whether varsity soccer looks viable for your teenager in the future.

Hitting the highs with varsity

Varsity soccer can bring the excitement of playing for the school and competing for championships. Being a varsity athlete is quite an achievement in itself in any sport.

Varsity soccer is not for the faint of heart. High-school soccer in most states is very competitive and physical. It is generally not renowned for a style of play that is particularly conducive for technical, skillful players to rule the roost. Traditionally, kids who have matured the most physically feature prominently on teams, and the training and tactics deployed by coaches often focus on winning versus developing skillful players.

REMEMBER

Keep this in mind. Your kid may thrive if they are relatively big and strong for their age. On the other hand, if your child is a smaller player but has great ball skills, high-school soccer may not be the best stage to maximize their playing time and develop skills.

If your child has made it to varsity soccer, they'll compete in regular season competition against local teams with the aim of making the playoffs.

Timing and exact structure vary by state for postseason competition, but in most cases the playoffs start with teams from regional areas competing and then if they advance, move on to state-level finals. There may also be different brackets within states depending on school size.

TIP

Whether or not your child wins a state championship, competing alongside their friends for school pride can certainly bring moments they'll remember forever. Whether it's the togetherness built by bus rides out to play a rival school or the pain or agony of a close game, there's certainly something special about school soccer.

4

Advancing in Elite Soccer

Navigate the alphabet soup of competing elite leagues and the pathways they promise.

Find out what to expect and what to do if your kid wants to pursue playing college soccer.

Sort through common challenges of playing at this level.

Consider options for exploring soccer abroad and the beauty of participating in the global game.

IN THIS CHAPTER

» **Assessing the opportunities and challenges of elite soccer**

» **Unpacking the alphabet soup of top competitions**

» **Getting noticed by elite academies**

Chapter **13**

Assessing Academy Soccer Programs

O nce your child reaches the under-13 age level, an additional pathway for top players opens up that's aimed at preparing and showcasing players for possible collegiate or professional play. This level is only for players who are extremely serious about soccer and willing — with your support and likely funding — to travel frequently across the country on a regular basis to play.

While terminology varies, these programs are often known as "academies" or sometimes as "elite." In this chapter, I guide you through the various top competitions for girls and boys if you think it may be right for your child to pursue that option.

Considering Academy Soccer

In this book, I've already covered the step up from recreational to competitive soccer, which brings with it a major commitment to the sport for your child and your family. The next step up to the highest tier of youth soccer in elite leagues requires even further commitment. This encompasses everything from significantly greater physical and mental demands on your child to materially larger outlays of time and money on participation (in most cases).

REMEMBER

Getting onto the top teams in each state is a very selective process — only a sliver of players in the youth soccer world in each age group make it. There are tons of highly competitive and fun soccer outside this tier that you can explore elsewhere in this book, so be sure to be realistic about where in the system your child may fit best.

The following sections let you know what you can expect if your family explores potentially trying out to play at the highest level of boys' or girls' competition.

Paving the way to college and the pros

The main reason for the existence of academy programs — the very highest levels of youth soccer in the country — is to develop and showcase youth players to move on to play college or (in much smaller numbers) professional soccer.

If your child isn't interested in potentially playing at that level after high school, there's probably not much point even exploring the programs discussed here. These programs are all extremely demanding, require extensive travel, and (with a few exceptions) demand high fees to participate.

REMEMBER

Playing in an elite academy does not guarantee your child will become a professional soccer player or get a full ride to a top college soccer program. Both of those scenarios only unfold for an extremely small number of players each year.

However, playing at this level certainly does increase the odds of getting recruited to college, and if your player happens to be an absolutely outstanding performer, of making it to the professional ranks. The chances of making it to these higher levels if your child isn't in an elite program are very slim indeed.

Academies provide credibility to scouts and coaches for players to make it onto their radar. They know only extremely good players will have made it to this level. Academies also provide exposure — college and professional scouts watch matches in academy play and especially tournaments.

Strong academic performance can also help open up a potential college team position for your player because the coach can get the player more academic money and not dip into their scholarship budget.

Again, none of this is a guarantee of any future opportunity happening at the even more competitive levels of college or professional soccer. For more on the process of getting recruited to college soccer, see Chapter 14.

Committing to academy soccer

Should your youth athlete have the desire to compete in college or even try to make it as a professional, these elite academy pathways are critical to understand. It's important, though, to be realistic about the potential your player has to make it at this level.

They need to be one of the top players at a very competitive level already to even be considered for academy programs. As well as their skill level, a strong level of fitness and mental focus to commit to the amount of play and travel required are needed to succeed.

Engaging in intense training and competition

There are no two ways about it: Playing at the top level of youth soccer means that playing this sport will have to come first over other social or sporting activities for much of your child's high school years. This is a sacrifice that should only be made out of a true love for the game as well as the ambition to compete at higher levels.

Training is essentially year-round, typically with four practices a week and games on weekends. The intensity of training is extremely high: Your athlete will be coached by the highest-level staff in youth soccer in the United States on an extremely competitive program to even get into.

That means there will be no latitude for missing practice without a good reason, being late, or slacking off in any way. The focus is entirely on elite development and success on the field. All of your player's teammates will be outstanding talents. A player who was a star on a good competitive team may be just one of the pack among a collection of the very best players in their region.

Similarly, matches will be at a very high intensity against consistently top-level competition. There are unlikely to be easy games. Even securing playing time could be a challenge: At this level, coaches focus on lineups that they think will produce the strongest results rather than trying to equalize playing time among players.

TIP

Talk through the reality of competing at this level with your young athlete. If you can, attend an academy's team practice or watch a game with your player before they commit to get a sample of the experience.

Traveling far and wide

If you thought regular travel soccer in club competitions already drained plenty of your time and money hauling your kid to play across the state or regionally, the top elite competitions will demand even more of you.

REMEMBER

The amount of travel varies drastically depending on your location. Clubs in areas with large populations and a strong elite youth soccer base may provide more convenient options for regular season games than clubs in areas located far from other metropolitan hotspots. Depending on your distance from other clubs, flying often on weekends during the regular season may be required.

Tournaments are also staged regionally and nationally that will almost certainly require out-of-state travel on multiple occasions throughout the year. The distance to travel depends on which tournaments your club participates in and where they are in relation to your own location, but it can often entail crisscrossing the country at least a couple of times for a full weekend's play.

Paying to play

Costs for participating in elite academies include registration fees, uniforms, travel costs, and a few other miscellaneous items. Much of this is similar to the costs for club soccer (see Chapter 5), with the major difference being much higher travel costs. Registration fees are also likely be slightly higher.

The cost of playing in elite academies varies wildly. For MLS Next academies that are part of parent Major League Soccer (MLS) teams, there is no cost for players to participate — a consistent rule across MLS club academies. The goal is to remove one of the barriers to entry in elite youth soccer: the cost of paying to play.

Most other clubs in MLS Next — which are not run by an MLS club — and in other leagues (see "Looking at the Elite Leagues" later in this chapter) do still charge significant registration fees.

All-in, depending on how far and frequently your club needs to travel for games, for most players the total cost of participation including travel and other expenses is typically between $10,000 and $15,000 a year.

WARNING

This is obviously a very significant amount of money, so be sure to go in with your eyes open if your athlete has the opportunity to participate in an elite academy.

Looking at the Elite Leagues

Because youth soccer isn't confusing enough, there are multiple top competitions at the U-13 to U-19 levels that compete separately in both the boys' and girls' spaces. There are also regional variances in which competition rules the roost. In this section, I offer a general overview of the top competitions nationwide with some tips on what the best option may be for your locale.

TIP

If you live in an area that doesn't offer top academies, take a look into your state's soccer association and consider try outs for their Olympic Development Program. This program also offers training in addition to their regular club team and participates in soccer showcases where college scouts attend and select players.

The top girls' competitions

There are two leading organizations on the girls' side of top-level youth soccer: the Girls Academy (GA) and the Elite Clubs National League (ECNL).

Both run extremely strong leagues at the U13 to U19 age levels and are the main "feeder" systems to recruitment for college soccer. The two entities compete with each other, vying to feature the top clubs in the country, and sometimes clubs move from one organization's leagues to the other.

>> **ECNL:** The ECNL was founded in 2009 as a national girls' competition, filling a void for a top pathway competition for elite players in the girls' game. It has steadily expanded since then, now boasting 128 teams across the country in its highest tier of play. The second tier, the ECNL Regional League, contains another 253 girls' clubs.

>> **Girls Academy:** The Girls Academy was founded in 2020. Its initial membership was filled by clubs who had previously been in an academy league — the US Soccer Development Academy — that was dissolved at that time.

The GA now has around 100 member clubs nationwide, playing in the U13 to U19 age groups. The clubs are divided into eleven regional conferences, playing a season that runs from August until the next summer, with playoffs and national championship events taking place in June and July.

Since ECNL and GA teams don't face each other in competition, it's difficult to gauge which entity is strongest overall. However, the general consensus is that ECNL has the edge on the strongest teams on the girls' side, with a particularly strong pipeline to college coaches for recruitment.

Soccer is always local, though: Your nearby GA team may be relatively strong while the ECNL club may be weaker.

The best boys' competitions

On the boys' side at the highest level of elite soccer, two organizations are dominant in securing the top teams and players across the country: MLS Next and the boys' version of the ECNL.

MLS Next

MLS Next, as the name suggests, is run by Major League Soccer, which has all of its professional teams participating through their elite academy programs.

MLS Next is not exclusive to MLS-affiliated teams, because the league simply doesn't cover enough territory or have enough youth players in the pipeline to be the best elite league nationwide with just its own teams. MLS Next features over 130 clubs that field almost 600 teams in the U13, U14, U15, U16, U17, and U19 age groups.

It's important to note that MLS Next's primary goal is to create a pipeline of talent to the professional game in the United States, though many graduates of the program do go on to play college or professional soccer overseas.

MLS Next plays a 10-month season, with 25–30 regular season games, plus additional winter and spring showcase tournaments along with postseason playoffs.

Players on MLS Next primary rosters are *not* permitted to play middle or high-school soccer, although players on ECNL teams are allowed to do so. MLS Next has an exception for this for players in private school who were accepted there based on their participation with the high-school soccer team.

ECNL

Though it was started eight years later than the girls' version, the boys ECNL program is similar to the girls ECNL program in serving as an elite pathway to college soccer. It features many of the top teams in the country, with more than 150 clubs participating on the boys' side.

ECNL clubs span the U13 to U19 age groups across 10 regional conferences. A big difference from MLS Next is that there are no restrictions on players also competing in high-school soccer, with the seasons designed to avoid overlap.

Though the seasons do not overlap, it can be challenging physically and mentally for players to compete in high-school soccer as well as ECNL. See Chapter 12, for more guidance.

Just as with ECNL and the GA on the girls' side, there is no unifying competition on the boys' side with both MLS Next and ECNL competing, so there is no guaranteed way of knowing which teams are truly the strongest nationally. However, there's no doubt both are elite competitions, with MLS Next having the edge in developing players toward the professional game and ECNL having a very strong reputation for the college pathway. Again, which academy is strongest depends on the situation in your local area.

Next-tier leagues

While ECNL and GA rule the roost for girls, and ECNL and MLS Next do the same for boys, there are additional leagues that feature elite talent such as USL Academies (if your area has a USL professional team). Depending on the richness of the local youth soccer talent, some teams' recruiting quality and coaching standards are as strong as those of some weaker teams at that top tier.

That's to say, if your child wants to be challenged at a high level but can't reach the very top, there are plenty of demanding competitions and high-level games and training they can participate in. Bear with me here, as I introduce more league names and alphabet soup to keep track of.

I've already covered the ECNL, which has top level play in both girls' and boys' formats. In 2016, ECNL added a second tier of play, ECNL Regional, which features more than 250 clubs on both the boys' and girls' sides. The level of play in ECNL Regional is certainly highly competitive, with many clubs proving their quality to the point that they have been promoted to the first-tier ECNL national league.

As the name suggests, ECNL Regional is regionalized play — at least in the regular season. Compared to the top tier of ECNL, this keeps travel somewhat more contained and affordable. Regional playoff events are also held, which additionally serve as showcases for college coaches to scout players. It's not all regional though: There are national finals for teams that qualify, meaning that travel to one central national location is possible.

Of course, it's not as simple as ECNL Regional having a monopoly at this tier of play just below the top elite leagues. On the girls' side, there's also the Development Player League (DPL). Connected to the top tier Girls Academy I discuss earlier, the DPL operates nationally with dozens of clubs across the country.

The Elite Academy League (EAL) on the boys' side is similar to the DPL on the girls, operating nationally. The EAL offers talent ID events aimed at helping players reach higher levels of play.

Meanwhile, the United States Youth Soccer operates the National League, which is generally considered a tier below and operates multiple competitions, including the Elite 64 and Premier 1.

Getting into the Elite Pathway

The percentage of youth soccer players that play on elite youth academy teams is very small. So what will elite academies be looking for and how can your player get on their radar? Read on.

The elite academy recruitment process

There are multiple pathways to ultimately getting offered a spot on an elite academy. Clubs will certainly be monitoring the performance of their high-level players as they develop in competitive programs, and exceptional performers will get flagged to try out for their own academy. This can come in the form of an invite to your player if they are spotted as a potential recruit for the academy.

Particularly in tournament play, coaches will also be on the lookout for top players at other clubs that they may want to recruit over to their academy program. Word of mouth about an unusual talent can also spread to coaches and program directors.

REMEMBER

This isn't always the case, though, especially for players who may not be participating in the traditional top levels of competitive youth soccer. There's no doubt that the general "pay-to-play" model in American youth soccer means much of the sport revolves around suburban play, with many players in urban areas often not being able to afford or access competitive clubs.

In those cases, or for players who may be strong enough but haven't made it onto academy scouts' radars for whatever reason — perhaps they may be later bloomers physically — many academies do hold open tryouts each year. You can register your player for these, and there is little harm in taking a shot: At the least, it'll be a few hours of good soccer for them to play.

TIP

Just be sure not to pile on the pressure, as relatively few players make it through open tryouts to an elite team with very limited roster spots likely available.

Skills and attributes

What will elite team coaches be looking for to fill their rosters with the best talent in their area?

>> **Soccer fundamentals:** Having mastery of the ball, being strong at all the core elements of the game, and being able to use both feet well are base requirements for elite players.

>> **Physical attributes:** Separation from the bulk of extremely good competitive soccer players can come from having

unusual speed, strength, size, or athleticism. (This can be controversial, as youth players obviously develop physically at different rates.) Also, a high level of physical fitness and stamina are desired to be able to withstand the demands of intense training and high-level games.

>> **Soccer intelligence:** Being technically and physically elite isn't enough to reach the very top level of youth soccer in any but the most unusual of cases. Coaches look for players who show strong tactical understanding of how to play and can anticipate and move themselves and the ball in advanced ways that separates them from the competition.

TIP

To help your child develop the skills needed to reach the top level, take a look at Part 3 of this book for many tips on how to get extra touches and training outside regular club practice. Almost every player at the top academies will have been playing extra soccer to sharpen their skills.

Chapter **14**

Aiming for College

The dream of playing college soccer — and getting a full scholarship ride to do so — has fueled many an investment by parents in travel soccer and extra private coaching. While full rides are rare, there are certainly many opportunities to play in college with partial scholarships often available. (That said, your investment in youth soccer shouldn't be made hoping to get a "return" in scholarship dollars — that's not how it works for most players.)

Getting onto a college roster is a highly competitive process with lots of nuances to getting onto the radar of coaches. It's also important to assess playing soccer alongside the all-important consideration of academics, the cost of attendance, and life in college beyond the playing field. Read on to understand the landscape of college soccer.

Finding the Right Level

Before exploring the logistics of applying for and potentially playing college soccer, it's helpful to cover the various levels and names of the competitions that college soccer programs participate in. These vary widely in terms of the quality of play, the degree of competitiveness for acceptance, the facilities offered, and the demands on student time for participation.

The top level of soccer in college that you may hear the most about, the NCAA Division 1 (often called "D1" for short), is only one of several levels even within the NCAA; there are also other competitions outside of the NCAA's auspices that are well worth considering.

The following sections explore the different levels of play that may be options for your youth player, from the elite to more recreational levels.

Competing in the NCAA

You've probably heard of the NCAA (the *National Collegiate Athletic Association*), the organization responsible for some of the biggest competitions in college sports, perhaps most famously March Madness in basketball.

The NCAA also organizes the leading soccer competitions among major colleges; it was founded back in 1959 on the men's side, with many hundreds of institutions participating. These competitions are divided by gender, and within the men's and women's programs into three tiers of play.

School rankings can be found on the NCAA website for all divisions in order to get a good understanding of roughly where any NCAA program falls into the hierarchy of play. For information on scholarships at NCAA schools, check out "Exploring Scholarships" later in this chapter.

NCAA Division I

There's no doubt that the NCAA D1 level is the peak of competition in college soccer and provides the most exposure for athletes along with the best facilities. Many D1 soccer players have gone on to play at the very highest levels of the sport in the women's and men's game.

As of 2024, there are 347 D1 women's soccer colleges and 205 men's soccer programs. These programs compete for a national championship in the College Cup (men's) and Women's College Cup.

Playing in Division 1 soccer requires an intense amount of commitment, and if your high school student is seriously aiming for this level, understanding this ahead of time will prepare them better for the experience. Not only do D1 teams train hard and frequently (often five times a week for multiple hours a day), extra conditioning work throughout the off season is also expected, and students need to come to the first practice each season in excellent shape. There can be no slacking off in the summer.

In addition to on-the-field training, early morning strength and conditioning sessions are usually held along with plenty of additional team meetings. Of course, there is a lot of travel to games on weekends.

REMEMBER

The college experience for a D1 athlete will be different than for a lot of their non-athlete peers: Partying frequently is not an option, and time to socialize in general is much more restricted than for non-athletes. Balancing academics and athletics will be a challenge, so it's important to understand the type of experience your athlete is looking for.

NCAA Division II

You might expect a big step down in the level of play and intensity for D2 soccer versus D1, but that's not necessarily the case. Many top D2 programs are seen to be close to or at the level of lower ranked D1 programs. One key difference is they are generally part of smaller schools — 93 percent of D2 schools have fewer than 10,000 students versus 44 percent at the D1 level.

REMEMBER

Given that D2 schools are usually smaller than D1 schools from a community and academic perspective, the D2 experience will be very different from that at a large, major public D1 college. Be sure to discuss with your prospective college student the type of experience they are looking to get beyond the soccer field. A D2 school may be a better fit depending on what they are looking for.

NCAA Division III

Most D3 NCAA schools are smaller, with only 2 percent having more than 10,000 undergraduate students and 77 percent having fewer than 3,000 students. They are often private, liberal arts institutions with a large focus on academics. This can often mean a higher cost of attendance than for D2 or D1 schools, and in terms of soccer, no athletic scholarships are available.

The demands of playing soccer in D3 schools is not quite as intense as in the higher NCAA tiers but it's still a substantial commitment. There is quite a wide variance in the level of play among D3 colleges, so if the competitiveness of the program is important for your student athlete, be sure to look carefully at the team's results and rankings.

NAIA, junior college, and club soccer

Outside of NCAA competition, there are still hundreds of other institutions to play collegiate soccer at that fall under different organizational auspices.

NAIA

The largest college athletic organization outside the NCAA is the *National Association of Intercollegiate Athletics* (NAIA), comprised largely of smaller college campuses than NCAA member schools.

The NAIA's national men's competition, the NAIA Men's Soccer Championship, is contested annually and dates back to 1959. The women's equivalent, the NAIA Women's Soccer Championship, was first held in 1984. There are almost 200 member colleges on both the women's and men's sides of NAIA competition. Rankings for NAIA teams can be found on the official NAIA website, www.naia.org.

TIP

NAIA schools distinguish themselves from NCAA programs by offering smaller, more collegiate campuses and a greater balance between athletics and academic life on campus. Many say there is less pressure than at high-level NCAA programs, leading to less stress around performing in soccer with a stronger community feel.

You may be wondering how the level of play in NAIA soccer compares to NCAA. Because teams from both competitions don't compete against each other outside of exhibition matches, it's difficult to judge exactly. Many experts suggest the top NAIA soccer teams are competitive with Division III or even some Division II programs in the NCAA.

Junior college

The two-year programs in junior college (also called community college) suffer from perception about their standing in the sports and academic world. However, they are still well worth considering for both cost-effective academic institutions and in soccer, as places to gain valuable playing time in the first two years of college.

The governing body for junior college soccer is the *National Junior College Athletic Association* (NJCAA), which has over 500 member institutions. Like the NCAA, it tiers sports programs into three divisions.

As you'd expect, Division 1 is the strongest and tiers down to Division 3. The top two divisions do offer athletic scholarship opportunities (see "Exploring Scholarships" later for more information). The level of play can be extremely strong at the top teams, though it can vary markedly around the country at the lower tiers.

REMEMBER

Junior colleges are two-year programs that lead to associate's degrees. From there, students either enter the workforce or transfer to a four-year college to complete their bachelor's degrees. For soccer players, the opportunity to transfer after showcasing skills at junior college can lead to places on NCAA or NAIA rosters.

Because junior colleges do not have juniors or seniors, freshmen and sophomores get a lot more playing time on the team than their peers at NCAA or NAIA four-year schools. This can allow for both more development on the field and the opportunity to prove and showcase skills for a transfer to a strong soccer program after two years. There are many cases of players from junior college transferring to excellent NCAA programs, including in D1.

Transferring to a four-year program also depends upon good academic performance and achieving a strong GPA. This can help with both potential academic and soccer scholarships.

TECHNICAL STUFF

For the Californians out there, junior college is different in the Golden State than in the rest of the country. California community colleges are members of a different athletic governing body exclusive to the state, the California Community College Athletic Association (CCCAA), so teams do not participate in NJCAA competition nor are athletic scholarships offered.

College club soccer

Perhaps your student doesn't want the pressure and intensity of high-level intercollegiate play, but does want to keep playing soccer at a good level and socialize with other players. When they're thinking about college, it can help to remind them that NCAA or NAIA play isn't the be-all and end-all to keep playing. Each year, many thousands of students enjoy playing what is known as "club soccer." These teams are not eligible for university sponsorships, don't take part in NCAA or NAIA competitions, and are often student-run organizations.

At some schools, though, the standard of club soccer is excellent. Many students who could have played NCAA soccer take part, either because they want to be at that particular school or because they don't want the intensity of high-level collegiate soccer. Most players on good club soccer teams have played high-school soccer or travel soccer before going to college.

TIP

Club soccer is a step above intramural soccer, another option for recreational play in college. Unlike intramural soccer, club soccer teams compete against clubs from other universities, and there is usually a selection process to get on the team.

The participation expectation of club soccer players is not as intense as for NCAA teams, but during the season it still requires multiple practices a week and games on weekends, including traveling to other colleges. Competition is organized into regional conferences.

REMEMBER

Club sport participation is truly done for the love of playing the game and the opportunity to make lasting friendships. If your student is considering college and wants to keep playing soccer but not at the most competitive levels, checking out a few college club soccer programs in advance can be a good way of knowing whether the school will be a nice fit to continue in the sport in this way.

Getting Recruited for College

Are you ready to help your student do a lot of extra homework to get on the radar of college coaches? Supporting your student athlete so that they can land at the best college possible takes a mix of showcasing their skills, thoroughly researching the options, and getting in touch with decision makers in the right way.

TIP

You can't — and shouldn't — do all of this work for your child. If they really want to play college soccer, it's important that they are driving the process, reaching out to coaches, and doing their own research. But your support will be invaluable to help them along the way.

It goes without saying that developing the right skill base and athletic qualities needed for college soccer is a bare minimum. If your child has only played recreational soccer, they are not going to land on even a D3 team.

A track record of performing at high-level club soccer is almost always a prerequisite for high-level NCAA programs. If your child has focused on high-school soccer and not club soccer, then the focus should probably go to NAIA or junior college programs to keep playing in college. See the earlier section "Finding the Right Level in College Soccer" for an overview of the various tiers of play.

Building a soccer reel and resume

Soccer coaches are inundated with outreach from prospective players. In order to have an impact when contacting coaches (see the later section "Contacting coaches via email"), your athlete will need materials to share that clearly showcase who they are and why the coach should pay attention to them. The core of this comes from a quick video the coach can watch of your player's highlights and a resume document providing a summary of their experience and attributes.

The point of a highlight reel

The best way to show prospective coaches a soccer player's skill — if they can't see it live in person — is by sharing a highlight reel that shows the range and quality your player has. This allows a coach to evaluate the player quickly, which may lead to an in-person scouting follow-up or at least get the player on their radar.

Filming footage

Some club or high-school teams may already film match footage and may use an online service such as Hudl that you can access, so ask your club or high school if this is happening already.

If you're filming the footage yourself, make sure you set up the camera on a tripod. Handholding the camera will result in shaky footage that will be hard to follow and unlikely to be watched by a coach.

TIP

Tripods with extensions that elevate the camera angle provide a much better view of the game for a coach to follow the play from. Think about broadcast coverage of professional sports — it's filmed from above instead of the ground level so viewers can better see what's happening. Alternately, you may be able to film from higher above the ground from a bleacher or mound surrounding the pitch.

Editing the best bits

The video should be around 3–5 minutes long and showcase positive highlights that portray the qualities of play your athlete really wants to emphasize. If the player is a defender, for example, lead with strong tackles or defensive plays versus showing a goal scored. Make sure to start the video with an intro of who the player is and then transition to the most impactful moments of play captured on video.

In the video, your athlete should be highlighted at the start of each clip with an arrow or circle so that the coach can identify them and follow their part in the play. Remember, the coach has no idea how to identify the player otherwise.

There is no need to add music to the video. Copyrighted music can result in a video being automatically detected and pulled down from a video-sharing website. And in any case, you have no idea what type of music any given college soccer coach might want to listen to — it's just a distraction.

How to save and send your highlight video

Video files are big, so it won't work to just send the video file as an attachment in an email. Instead, you can upload it to an online video storage website such as Vimeo or YouTube. You'll need to sign up for a free account on either service to upload the video.

When saving a video on YouTube or Vimeo, look for the setting to make the video private. You can then send the link to the video for access to only those who need it, such as the coaches you're sharing it with. Your athlete will want to include a link to the video in the first outreach to college coaches. Make sure that all the coach needs to do is click on the video to watch it, without having to go through any other steps to download or login to view the footage.

Crafting a resume

Your athlete will also need a soccer-focused resume that can give coaches the ability to quickly scan an overview of their experience, attributes, achievements, and coaches as references.

On the resume, the following info should be included; verify that your athlete's resume has this covered:

>> **Basic info:** Name, age, soccer position, address, high school, contact information.

>> **Attributes:** Key abilities, height, weight.

- **Experience:** Current and past clubs, leagues, tournaments, and camps participated in, plus notable achievements (individual and team). Be sure the names and locations of these are clear.

- **Academics:** High school, advisor name and contact information, GPA, and any honors/achievements.

- **Other activities:** Additional languages, sports clubs, extramural activities, and interests.

Make sure the resume document is saved as a PDF document and is formatted with clear, easy-to-read fonts and spacing.

College showcases

Getting in front of college coaches and scouts in-person — having them see your athlete performing on the field — is a critical opportunity in the college recruiting process. So important is it, in fact, that special "showcase" events and tournaments are held each year to give high-school-age students the chance to get in front of an array of coaches and scouts.

Highly competitive teams typically enter tournaments that also serve as college showcase events. Which tournaments clubs enter depends on a number of factors, most importantly which competition they are part of. Head to Chapter 13 to read up on all the various elite programs and competitions.

Contacting coaches via email

Email is without doubt the best way to contact a college coach — they spend a lot of time in their inboxes. Your player should start their outreach by sending an email to the coach, introducing themselves. The email should be concise, polite, and provide the key basic information about their soccer credentials. The email subject line should include your player's graduating year, position on the field, and location, and state that you're including a highlight video reel. For example: "Center-back, Class of 2027: Tom Dunmore, Denver, CO, View Video."

The body of the email should start with a quick overview of basic information: the position the player plays, key skills, location, club/school, relevant soccer stats (for example, goals scored or assists), and soccer achievements. Scholastic ability (GPA) and notable extracurricular activities are important to include as well. And of course, a link to the highlight reel should be included.

TIP

Most college showcases post a list of college coaches who will be in attendance. This provides an opportunity for your player to send an email to a prospective college coach and let them know what game they will be playing in, what field, what time, and their player number.

Exploring Scholarships

First of all, it's important to set expectations with your student athlete about the availability and financial value of college scholarships in soccer. Even in a D1 program, "full rides" — scholarships that cover all the expenses related to attending college — are extremely rare.

In soccer, most scholarships are partial, meaning they cover only a portion of the cost of tuition (and nothing toward other expenses related to attending college). The value of these scholarships varies widely among colleges and between genders. In general, the dollar value of scholarships for female athletes is higher than for male athletes. Either way, it's worth keeping in mind that scholarships, if available at all, will likely range from $8,000 to $15,000 per academic year. Scholarships are offered by D1 and D2 programs in the NCAA but not D3 programs. NAIA and NJCAA programs also offer scholarships.

TIP

The cost of tuition at each college should be factored in when considering the amount of any partial scholarship offer: Private schools are typically much more expensive than in-state colleges, so even if a scholarship offer is higher from a private school, the total cost of attending college there could be much larger.

IN THIS CHAPTER

» Looking at coaching strategies and
how they impact players

» Handling playing time issues the
right way

» Talking about switching teams

Chapter **15**

Dealing with Challenges

I f your child is playing competitive soccer, you've already navigated a lot of questions and spent plenty of time (and money!)
on the sport. Balancing school life, social life, and other activities with soccer isn't straightforward — and those are just the
logistical challenges.

In this chapter, you get a look at a lot of the challenges that
come up surrounding playing on the field. Coaches are key to
your player having a good experience — perhaps, in fact, the
most important element of all. So I help you understand coaches
and how to work with them on issues such as playing time.
Finally, you will look at the options and what to keep an eye on
if soccer suddenly feels like a chore because it's not working out
on the field or because the amount of play and pressure is all
too much.

Understanding Coaching Approaches

As a parent, watching your child play and hearing your child's feedback, it sometimes can be difficult to take a step back and see the perspective a coach must have to manage 15 or so other kids on top of your own.

You, of course, see more of your young player's perspective, watching their every move and being attuned to what they think about how a practice or game has gone.

It's important to understand how coaches plan for and manage their teams across different styles, and to know how and when to talk to them directly on various questions or issues that may arise.

Considering coaching style and strategy

This may sound too basic, but the coach is there to coach — and almost every coach, especially in competitive soccer, will have a strategy and reasoning behind their approach that may not be obvious to you.

I talk a lot in this book about how important it is for your child for the focus to be on enjoying playing the game and developing better skills. To achieve these goals, a good coach may be working on developing either individual skills or team tactics that may take time to be effective. In the short term, this can result in frustration for a player and often, by association, for their parent.

For example, the coach may put into practice a style of play for the team that takes time for the players to practice and implement effectively in a game. Perhaps the coach wants the team to learn how to play the ball from the goalkeeper with a series of short passes up the field instead of the easier option of having the goalkeeper boot the ball as far as they can.

This type of strategy can be challenging for the team to adopt and may at first result in missed passes, losing possession, and even conceding goals that may not have happened with a long punt. But over time, the team may settle into playing this way well and benefit from learning how to possess the ball. This is a long-term benefit of a strategy that may, in the short term, produce concern among the players and parents while working through the kinks.

The lesson here is that there is often a method to a coach's approach and patience can be required of everyone to get to the best end result.

A coach can also change their team's style of play during a game based on what's occurring on the field. Every coach has a different style of coaching.

Playing with positions

Coaches are juggling how to fit an entire team of players into the right positions on the field and develop their skills. Not every player can always play their preferred, favorite position. A central midfielder may be asked to drop back in the team and play in defense at center back. There can be a myriad of reasons a coach may do this: It may be out of necessity or it may be that they strongly value this player's defensive abilities and need to maximize them for the benefit of the team.

In fact, it can actually be beneficial for a player to try a new position, even if it feels uncomfortable at first. Over time, the player may come to enjoy playing a different role and may even adopt it as their long-term spot.

Even if the player doesn't end up fitting into that role long-term, there is plenty of history in soccer to show that, for young players in particular, experiencing the opportunity to play different roles improves their all-around skills in the game and understanding of tactical play.

Patience, once again, is necessary here as it can take several games and weeks of practice to adapt to a new role and get comfortable. The short-term frustration a player feels should eventually dissipate.

REMEMBER

Like teachers, most coaches have been there and done this before, many times over, with whatever strategy they are adopting. Unlike with school, as parents we are there watching the process unfold at games, so we often feel more directly the emotions and difficulties of adapting to something new. But while there are certainly cases of coaches getting things wrong, a good general rule is to try to understand the goal of their approach and encourage your child to stick with it and give it a fair chance to reap benefits.

When to chat to the coach

All of that said, sometimes you will need to speak to the coach about what is happening with your player. After all, your child is investing a lot of their time into being part of the team.

WARNING

Don't go to a coach right after the game to question them, and don't go to the coach at the half. Allow 48 hours after the game to elapse before asking a question to let emotions dissipate. Be prepared for an answer you may not want to hear. Understand that the coach has multiple players (and multiple parents) to manage. Avoid negative discussions about coaching or any other players on the team.

There are many reasons to speak to the coach to address issues, but a good way to approach it is to start with a spirit of positive inquiry. That's to say, if you want to find out more about the coach's approach to the game, or have a general question about soccer that (somehow!) this book doesn't answer, any good coach should be happy to chat to a parent. In fact, they'll likely be pleased with the interest!

There may be times when you have more particular questions about the coach's approach and tactics, perhaps related to some of the topics I discuss earlier: Maybe you're wondering why your player is in a certain role or why the team is approaching the game in a certain way.

Proactively asking about tactics and player development strategies in order to understand them and help your child realize the reason behind the coach's approach can be helpful. However, it's important not to approach the coach by questioning their decisions, pushing for your child to do something different than they have decided, or criticizing other kids on the team.

A spirit of inquiry to find out more is a positive approach to take when approaching the coach. If instead, negative emotions are on display — perhaps because a parent is upset that their player got substituted early or wasn't selected to start — all that is likely is a confrontation rather than a conversation that can actually provide any positive insights.

The challenges discuss here reflect issues around the play on the field and not any player safety concerns that may be impacting anyone physically or mentally in a potentially abusive fashion. These serious issues should be dealt with following the channels I outline in Chapter 7.

Tackling Playing Time Issues

How "fair" the coach is being with playing time is a very difficult subject to navigate. They must balance developing players with the pressure on the team to perform on the field, and these priorities vary depending on the level of play and intention of the program your child is in.

First things first: Considering your child's place in the pyramid

Before diving into how to address playing time issues, it's critical to consider the club your player is in and where it fits into the soccer playing pyramid. This part of the book is aimed at parents of children in advanced competitive programs, where playing time at the higher levels is often distributed unevenly with the intent to win games. For an overview of recreational soccer and starter levels of competitive soccer, where playing time should be equally balanced across the team, see Parts 1 and 2.

Even at more competitive levels of play — which may have names such as "select," "premier," "elite," or "academy" — there will be gradations of just how heavily selection by the coach should be based on performance and the goal of winning versus developing all the players on the field. This may even vary within the season itself: In regular season games, playing time may be more evenly distributed than in tournament play, when the stakes are higher and coaches (and programs) are looking to garnish their reputations with trophy wins.

TIP

When heading into the season, aim to set expectations with your kid on how competitive securing playing time will be. This is especially important if your player is advancing to a more selective and challenging level of player, where it's more likely playing time may be weighted around tactical and performance plans by the coach instead of giving every player the same amount of playing time.

When playing time disappears

There's a big difference between a coach making some adjustments among players for time on the field to tweak performance goals and simply sitting players for most of or even entire games.

Frankly, there is no reason in youth soccer for a player not to see a reasonable amount of minutes on the field. Every player deserves the opportunity to play and develop; that is, after all, the purpose of youth sports. Perhaps, at the very oldest levels of youth play and at the most competitive level, the argument can be made that limiting playing time may be acceptable. But even then, it speaks to poor roster construction if a player isn't deemed good enough to suit up.

The damage done to a young player sitting on the bench most of a game can be significant emotionally as well as impeding their development as a player. It can feel embarrassing or even humiliating to know that your coach doesn't appear to trust you to contribute to the team. Unfortunately, this scenario happens too often, including (or perhaps even especially) in elite tournament play. This exacerbates the challenge for a parent who has likely spent considerable time and money to take their child on a travel team, perhaps even to another state, for them then to play barely a few minutes on the field.

REMEMBER

If this is happening to your child, it's an issue to address with the coach first before considering other options. Limited minutes should be a particular concern at younger ages, but even at older ages or on a highly competitive team, your child won't gain much by sitting on the bench.

TIP

When approaching the coach about this issue, similar to the guidance I note earlier about starting from a positive angle, it's helpful to start with a proactive approach: Ask to understand the coach's perspective and whether there are things your player can work on to earn more playing time. Be open minded about what the coach tells you. Playing time may be a result of various factors that they should explain to you.

In an ideal scenario, the coach's explanation helps give context to the decisions and a pathway is laid out for your player to gain significantly more minutes. What if the coach's response isn't helpful or nothing changes after a couple of more games? At that point, unfortunately, it may be worth exploring the following options — switching to another team within the club, or even looking to switch clubs entirely. The first step is to look at your club's communication tree and escalate your concerns in an appropriate manner.

Exploring Other Teams

There are positive, negative, and neutral reasons to explore moving to another team, many of which are covered in Chapter 6, especially around moving from less to more competitive teams. This section looks at moving up, sideways, or down in the soccer pyramid to solve a challenge on the field.

Moving on up at the elite level

Sometimes your player's ceiling may be limited by the team or club they are currently on. For more on the process of moving up and considering open competitive tryouts, see Chapter 6. However, it's important to note that most of the top elite outfits such as MLS Next or ECNL teams (see Chapter 13 for a look at the landscape of top clubs) offer tryouts on an invite-only basis to players from their current clubs or from other clubs.

Many clubs have a form that parents or players can submit to express their interest in trying out for an elite team. These forms gather basic information about your player's age, gender, and location, but more importantly, they ask which club and league they are currently playing in.

Usually, top-level clubs are interested in looking at players at the highest levels of their current club. For high school age players, they may also ask for a video of highlights of their play.

REMEMBER

Submitting the form doesn't guarantee a tryout will be offered, but it at least flags your player for the coaching staff to consider. You'll hear back via email if they want your player to join the tryout.

Finding a new opportunity

The rest of this section looks at the need to potentially switch teams from the perspective of doing so to address a real challenge your child is having on their current team. This issue may need to be solved by either moving horizontally across to another team at a similar level or considering moving down a level.

This may be for a myriad of reasons: It may be the playing time issue or coach challenges mentioned earlier.

TIP

Your child getting good playing time to enjoy the experience and developing their skills is more important than the "status" of what team they are on — which no one will remember in the years to come.

If your child has been moved up to a level that they are not competitive enough for, it may be better to move down a level to get more playing time. Your player's coach is the best place to start this conversation, but you can also speak to the club's director of coaching if needed: Remember, they are likely to want to keep your child in the club (player fees pay the bills!), so they will want to find a solution to level up your player's experience appropriately.

TIP

The simplest solution is certainly to switch teams within the same club, assuming that they offer multiple levels of play. Changing clubs may bring logistical challenges if the location for practices or games isn't as convenient.

There's also a challenge to switching to another club entirely during the season. You may already have paid the fees for the season at your child's current club; it's usually not possible to recoup those fees if you leave, and then you will need to pay the fees at a new club.

The most logical time to change clubs, then, is at the end of the season before registration is due for the next year. This is the time you can shop around, assuming that there are multiple club options in your area. See Chapter 6 for information about trying out for another club.

If the issues with your current club are so extreme that you need to make an in-season change, there are a couple of things to consider in addition to fees:

» You may need to work with your current and future club to have your player's registration with the state association adjusted to a new club. Contact your local state association for information about how this works in your area.

» Since tryouts aren't likely being held during the season by any other club, you need to contact other clubs and see if you can arrange an invitation to try out with them. This may mean an invite to come to a couple of regular team practices and join in.

Chapter **16**

Exploring Soccer Overseas

U nlike the other big sports in America — football, baseball, basketball, and ice hockey — in the case of soccer, the pinnacle of the sport isn't on this continent. Soccer is truly a global game, so you not only find the best soccer to watch overseas but also opportunities for your child (or young adult) to experience playing overseas — something they may be particularly interested in if playing at advanced levels.

This chapter gives you a basic overview of the sport globally to get you set if you venture overseas with your soccer-mad kid to experience it firsthand. Read on as I take a look at "Planet Soccer."

Although I give you a few basics about Planet Soccer here, I also suggest that you consider looking up a copy of *Soccer For Dummies* (which your author may have some responsibility for!) — a comprehensive guide to the game as a fan.

Looking Around Planet Soccer

If you didn't grow up as a fan of soccer, as many in America did not, coming to grips with the "world's game" may seem daunting. There are professional soccer leagues all over the globe and the sport has a long, deep history.

TIP

Don't be daunted — millions of people in America have discovered the sport as adults, often because their kid has taken up the sport. While you can guide your kid's soccer experience just fine without knowing which team won the English Premier League last year, getting into the sport can definitely add some more context and enjoyment to all the time you'll spend around it as a soccer parent.

And if you're considering sending your kid on an overseas camp or tour, as I cover later in this chapter, it's good to know a bit about the sport worldwide.

The "Big Leagues" in global soccer

Although North America's NBA, NFL, MLB, and NHL are unmatched and dominant leagues in their respective sports globally, the same isn't quite true for American soccer leagues' prestige and standing globally.

The top women's leagues

In women's soccer, America's National Women's Soccer League (NWSL) certainly can lay a strong claim to being one of the strongest leagues in the world. After all, the U.S. Women's National Team has long been one of the best in the world, and there's a strong pipeline of talent that feeds into domestic American clubs.

And on the flip side of that, women's soccer was often sadly an afterthought for big European soccer clubs, with few resources put into youth development for girls or the professional game.

That has started to change in recent decades, with new top-tier professional leagues starting in places like England and countries like Spain producing some of the best players in the world.

The top women's club teams in the world outside of the United States play in the UEFA Women's Champions League, which for the past decade has been dominated most recently by Barcelona of Spain and previously by Lyon of France.

The leading men's leagues

Modern soccer with the rules that are largely followed today was invented in Great Britain in the 19th century, codified into rules that were exported alongside traders venturing around the world at the peak of the British Empire's global expansion.

While Britain may be the original home of football, and England's Premier League is the most commercially successfully in the world, the sport has taken incredibly deep roots across the world in a way that's unmatched by any other sport.

It's worth name-checking some of the top leagues and teams, as these will often pop up even in youth soccer. Many European and South American teams have academies, camps, and tour programs that you may hear about in youth soccer targeted at American kids.

European leagues dominate the soccer world in terms of the television media rights revenue it generates, and hence the pay it can provide to attract the top stars.

The biggest leagues in Europe are considered to be England's Premier League, Spain's La Liga, Germany's Bundesliga, and Italy's Serie A — with France's Ligue 1 not far behind.

Within those leagues, there are a handful of teams in each who make up the elite, most followed clubs in world soccer, with rich histories of winning silverware and featuring superstar players.

A few of the top team names to know from those countries are Spain's Real Madrid, Atletico Madrid, and FC Barcelona; England's Manchester United, Liverpool FC, Chelsea, Arsenal, and Manchester City; Italy's Internazionale, AC Milan, and Juventus; Germany's Bayern Munich and Borussia Dortmund; and France's Paris Saint-Germain.

TIP

It's worth looking up those teams, as the names may appear not only in casual conversation around the soccer field, but also because many of them will operate summer camps or even full training camps in your area. See Chapter 11 for the skinny on the offerings from overseas clubs.

Contests on the international scene

Because soccer is truly a global sport, the World Cup has become a major event, with the men's version the most-watched sporting competition in the world.

Every four years in both men's and women's soccer (though on separate cycles a year apart), the top teams to have qualified compete to win the World Cup. I won't try to cover the long histories of World Cup tournaments here — again I recommend taking a peek at *Soccer For Dummies* — but suffice it to say that they are events worth tuning in to and a great way to rally the family behind supporting your nation.

TIP

The 2026 men's FIFA World Cup will be heading to North America, co-hosted by the United States, Mexico, and Canada. This will be a generational opportunity to see this event in person on our own shores and is certain to inspire your kid's love of the game to new heights. At the time of writing, tickets were not yet on sale, but you'll be able to find all the relevant information at the website of the governing body and organizer of the event, FIFA, at www.fifa.com.

As well as the World Cup, lots of other international contests take place between countries. Each nation plays exhibition games as well as continent-based competitions such as the European Championships (for, well, Europe) and Copa America for South America (slightly confusingly, the United States men's team often takes part in this competition).

Taking in the Sights — and Soccer

Maybe it's on your bucket list to do some sightseeing in Barcelona, London, or Paris, and maybe your kid would love to play soccer in another country. In that case, an international soccer tour might just check off two boxes at once and be a ton of fun for the whole family.

All-inclusive tours similar to sightseeing tours you may hear about for overseas vacations are available in most major soccer city destinations. Often you can find options for multi-city or even multi-country tours.

These tours usually do all the planning for you, arranging for sightseeing days and stadium tours of the top soccer venues, while your youth soccer player will likely take part in a soccer training camp and potentially play matches with local teams.

For example, you may go on a trip to Barcelona, which would include seeing the sights, sampling the local food, and visiting the famous Camp Nou stadium (home of Barcelona, one of the greatest teams in world soccer), alongside of soccer training sessions and games for your kid.

In most cases, everything is arranged, from airport transfers to sightseeing buses along with meals and accommodations. It's a turnkey experience to see a new part of the world and experience soccer culture elsewhere.

Tours usually last seven to ten days, with a sample itinerary looking something like this:

Day 1: Departure from the United States

Day 2: Arrival at European airport, transfer to accommodation

Day 3: Sightseeing in city, afternoon training

Day 4: Morning training, afternoon sightseeing, evening game

Day 5: Morning training, afternoon sightseeing, evening game

Day 6: Transfer to another city

Day 7: Morning sightseeing, afternoon training, evening game

Day 8: Morning training, afternoon sightseeing

Day 9: Morning sightseeing, evening game

Day 10: Transfer to airport, return flight to the United States

The cost of a tour varies according to the country being visited, the length of the trip, and the number of cities being visited. Trips in the spring are also a bit cheaper than during peak travel time in the summer.

TIP

Make sure to check whether prices offered by tour operators cover all the various costs including meals, accommodations, and especially airfare as this can be significant for intercontinental travel. Some operators include airfare in the listed tour fee (and have special deals with airlines), though taxes and other fees may be additional charges.

Exploring Overseas Soccer Culture

Traveling abroad can give you an opportunity to explore different soccer cultures, even if the primary purpose of a trip overseas is for other family vacation and sightseeing purposes.

If your kid is into soccer, taking a day to go to a match or do a stadium tour at a historic venue can provide a glimpse into the passion and history of the sport in other parts of the world.

The easiest way to do that is with soccer-specific tours (see the preceding section), but there are plenty of opportunities to take in some soccer on the side of a regular vacation abroad, depending on where you go.

You can find soccer around and about most towns or cities in the world, but for the purpose of keeping it simple and based around seeing some of the most memorable spots, I assume here that you're visiting an area close to one of the hotspots of world soccer culture Americans most often head to — places such as Italy, Spain, or England.

Touring the top spots

In those countries and many others around the world that feature historically famous teams, especially if you're pressed for time, a stadium tour of one of the grand old venues can be a relatively efficient but very rewarding way to soak in some vibes and heritage of the global game.

For example, on a visit to Rome you can book a visit to the Stadio Olimpico (Olympic Stadium), a historic venue opened in 1937 that has hosted the World Cup (in 1990) and — hence the name — the Olympic Games (in 1960). Booking a guided tour will let you see inside the venue, including going inside the locker rooms, seeing the trophy cabinet, and even stepping down to the pitch.

Tours of stadiums such as this or the Wembley Stadium in London or Camp Nou in Barcelona are usually run by a knowledgeable guide to take you around, sometimes with an audio headset companion piece. Tours typically last 60–90 minutes and can be booked in advance for set times of the day so that you can work them into your schedule.

TIP

Tour prices vary, but for a major European venue, expect to pay somewhere around $30 to $40 for the tour, with discounted prices for children.

Heading to a game

Of course, seeing an empty stadium isn't quite the same thing as taking in the sights and sounds of a live soccer match overseas. Fortunately, thousands of top-level professional matches take place every weekend, so there's no shortage of action overseas to catch.

There's an important caveat to that: Professional soccer leagues run seasonally (like American sports do), so there are breaks in between when games don't take place.

In major European soccer nations, this break takes place during the summer (usually in June and July), which is unfortunately when many from America head abroad on summer vacation. Some leagues also have a winter break.

You may still be able to find some live action, possibly with an international competition taking place, or an exhibition game in preseason.

Assuming that you are traveling during the season, you can find schedules for all leagues and teams on their websites or on a dedicated soccer app. See Chapter 19 for some tips on how to keep up with worldwide soccer matches from your phone.

Once you've found a match that aligns with your schedule, you need to figure out two important details: how you'll get to the game and how you'll secure tickets prior to attending.

Getting to the stadium

Of course, we can't give detailed directions to the thousands of stadiums across the world here: You'll need to look up the venue and see if the home team website gives directions for how best to get there, or utilize a tool such as Google or Apple Maps.

Just bear in mind that most stadia outside the United States aren't typically accessed by car with the sea of parking lots most NFL venues feature. Usually, a bus or train is the best way to get there.

Accessing tickets

Make sure you have secured your tickets before going to the match. Many teams sell out their games, and there's nothing worse than heading to a venue and being unable to get in. The way to purchase tickets also varies widely from team to team and country to country.

TIP

It's important to be aware of two things, however. In much of the rest of the world, including major soccer countries such as Italy or England, it's illegal to sell tickets above face value. This policy is positive in the sense that it limits price gouging around tickets, but it does mean that you can't expect to just find tickets on secondary ticket market websites like you can in the United States.

WARNING

Be very wary of purchasing tickets from any website other than the home team's official website. Many dubious sites claim to sell tickets that often end up being counterfeit. Because of the strict restrictions on the resale of tickets, you should be very dubious that purchasing tickets from an unauthorized vendor is genuine (and it may also be illegal).

TIP

If you're confused about the process of buying tickets to the team or venue you want to go to, you can always email or call them prior, and you'll usually find some customer service helpful for tourists.

What to expect at the match

It's fair to say that the experience at soccer games around the world is not as uniform as attending a baseball game at a major league venue in North America. Some venues are brand-new and will feel a lot like going to an NFL game. Tottenham Hotspur Stadium in London certainly does (and it is actually also an NFL venue for games held there annually).

However, other older stadiums feel worlds away, with fewer options for concessions. This can be a great thing, with plenty of charm and a different cultural approach to the game to appreciate.

While there may not be massive concourses with hundreds of food and drink options there, you may find instead a whole end of the stadium draped in flags; fans bouncing up and down throughout the game, singing for their team; and even fireworks going off inside the venue set off by the fans themselves (this section with the most boisterous fans is best viewed from a distance for the casual attendee).

You may have heard over the years about the dangers in European or South American soccer venues from hooligans. While there's no denying crowd violence has marred many games and cultures, contributing to some terrible human disasters, most top-level matches in countries such as Germany, England, or Spain are very safe to attend.

Despite this, there is one rule you should follow: Don't wear the colors of the away team or cheer for them unless you are specifically ticketed for and sitting in the "away" fans section of the stadium. This is a big no-no. Verbal abuse is almost certain to come your way, and passions run high in many games and rivalries; it's not worth risking it and ruining your family vacation.

With that heavier stuff out of the way, it's worth reiterating that heading to a game with your kid can be an experience of a lifetime and can really inspire them to love the game they play even more. The excitement and atmosphere at most venues is thrilling.

Don't forget to stop in the club shop at the stadium and pick up a bit of memorabilia — a scarf is the classic soccer accessory — to keep and remember 90 minutes of soccer a lot different from what you and your family may have ever seen.

5

The Part of Tens

Take a look at ten star players your child may want to follow.

Try out ten ways to get better at soccer at home.

Check out ten key points to help you understand the world's most popular sport.

Chapter **17**

Ten Star Players to Inspire Your Child

Every soccer fan ends up having a favorite player, so as your kid gets into the sport, they'll start to look around at stars on the top teams. This chapter offers a fun — but by no means exhaustive or especially objective — list of players who are prominent in the sport and fun to follow. This list may end up being as informative and helpful for you as for your child. As you're learning the sport, you can pick up plenty of inspiration from looking up the players on this list.

Since most of the players on this list are among the most famous athletes in the world, you can easily find highlights on YouTube and plenty of great articles online to read up on them.

Aitana Bonmatí

Spanish star Aitana Bonmatí has now won all the accolades at an individual and team level. She's won the world's best player award twice (the Ballon d'Or and winner of the World Cup with

Spain, among many achievements). Yet, observing what makes Bonmatí so great takes a little bit more study than many of the highlight-reel names on this list. It's worth taking your time with your child to dig a little deeper into how she plays to understand what makes her contributions to the game special.

Bonmatí makes her teams tick with an incredible ability to be the link between defense and attack, finding space with the ball and passes to the right player with an incredible consistency and accuracy.

How does she do this, and what lesson is there for your developing player? Bonmatí "scans" the play around her with a frequency and consistency that most players don't match. That means she is constantly looking around *before* she is passed the ball, so she already knows the array of options available and can select the best one. Bonmatí knows where her teammates are and where they are going, and she knows where the opposing players are and when she should either run with the ball into space or pass it to take advantage of any gaps they have left.

Getting to Bonmatí's level is, of course, not realistic. But there's a great simple lesson for any young player to work on looking around, scanning the players, and improving their anticipation.

Mary Earps

"Mary, queen of stops" is a fitting nickname for one of the great shot-stoppers in the world. The England goalkeeper has twice won FIFA's Best Women's Goalkeeper award (in 2022 and 2023) and was also named the best goalkeeper of the 2023 Women's World Cup, leading England to the final (losing at that stage to Spain).

Beyond the individual and team accolades, Earps stands out for her consistency and leadership. On the field, this shows in her organizing and communication with the defenders in front: a great example for any aspiring goalkeeper to understand the importance of directing play vocally in this position.

Off the field, Earps has not been afraid to speak up on many issues, including mental health and well-being, using her platform as one of the most prominent players in the sport for bigger causes.

Ederson

It used to be that goalkeeping was mostly about the hands; saving the ball from going in the net is, of course, the priority for the player in that role. That has started to change over time, with goalkeepers now more and more important in how they play a part in distribution of the ball with both hands and feet.

Few goalkeepers exemplify this trend more than Brazil's Ederson (formal name Ederson Santana de Moraes, but always known as just Ederson), whose role in galvanizing attacks as a goalkeeper has helped redefine the position. This comes from a mix of accurate short and long passes, particularly at club level, helping Manchester City's machine of outstanding possession constantly run at levels rarely seen in the game.

Ederson is a great player to study for young keepers to see that it's almost as important to develop their skills with their feet as with their hands.

Lindsey Horan

"Captain America" is not the most obvious selection on this list: The U.S. Women's National Team star and captain (as of this book's publication in 2025) isn't the fastest on her team, or the best finisher, or the best dribbler. That is, however, why she is on this list to inspire your child. Not every kid has the natural athletic skills or technique to dominate because of the one or two attributes they possess.

Although Horan has plenty of technical skill and athletic ability, she stands out among her peers and earned selection among an array of talented peers to captain the United States team for her determination, leadership skills, and game awareness. This is a great example for your young player to watch and learn from: Observe how she inspires and leads her teammates, plays smart and energetic soccer from her midfield role, and has become one of the best players around through hard work and dedication to the game.

Kylian Mbappe

Speed, power, dribbling ability, scoring goals — French superstar Kylian Mbappe is a human highlight reel whose incredible feats with the ball can't fail to get any kid excited to watch. Who doesn't want to run past defenders and smack the ball into the corner of the goal past a flailing goalkeeper? Nobody in men's soccer does that better than Mbappe. Just pull up a YouTube highlight reel of his performance in the 2022 World Cup final to see him pull this off on the biggest stage of them all.

If this type of player doesn't inspire your kid to get out there and start whacking the ball at the goal in the hope of being the next Mbappe, I'm not sure what can.

There's also a nuance to Mbappe's play you can point out that may help more advanced players think about how they approach the game. For all his speed and dynamism, what sets him apart from many others who are also lightning quick and strong is Mbappe's composure. Mbappe is able to control the ball even at high speed, not letting the ball run away from him. This is easier said than done, but it's a great example to try to copy!

Lionel Messi

Messi is the men's soccer GOAT. Fans of Portugal's Ronaldo — or older aficionados who may fairly point to past geniuses like Pele or Diego Maradona — might disagree about that designation, but in the purely subjective opinion of this author, it's Messi.

Why Messi? The Argentinian, who starred for Barcelona most of his club career and led his country to a World Cup title in 2022, is not only a serial winner, an incredibly prolific goal-scorer, and creator of chances for others, but he also does it with an élan and mesmerizing style few in the game have ever approached.

Messi is also proof that soccer is a game that can be dominated by players of any size. Standing 5'7" on a good day, Messi reminds us that a low center of gravity can be as beneficial as height or strength is in basketball or American football. So if your child happens to be average size or below, have them take a look at Messi to remind them that it's what you can do with the ball, not how tall you stand over it, that can make all the difference.

Christian Pulisic

There's only one American man on the list (there are two American women, which is fair as the U.S. Women's National Team has long been far more successful than its male counter-part). But Pulisic is the type of player any young American kid can look up to — starring in the top European leagues (currently for AC Milan) and having the technical skill to play comfortably alongside some of the best players in the world.

American male players don't always have an easy path to the top: Pulisic's persistence, versatility, and commitment playing at several clubs in Europe to make it to the top serve as a great inspiration for following your dream, however hard it may be to get there.

Alexia Putellas

Two-time winner of the Ballon d'Or as the best player in the world, Putellas (often known simply as Alexia) has been an inspirational force in midfield at the heart of the incredible rise of Spanish women's soccer in the past decade. She has starred for Barcelona at club level and Spain in the international game, winning every major honor available to her.

Putellas is a dream to watch for any player looking to learn how to play as a creative fulcrum for their team: Watch how she finds space with the ball, quickly connects play, and creates chances for her teammates. She links attack and defense with vision and intelligent movement, always keeping defending players on their toes.

Rodri

Rodri (full name Rodrigo Hernández Cascante, but always known just as Rodri) has shown that fans and the media can truly appreciate the type of player who makes a team tick and win games without being the flamboyant star of the show, claiming the Ballon d'Or as the world's best player in 2024. That same year, he also won another Premier League title with Manchester City and the European Championship national team crown for Spain.

Rodri has achieved all this playing a "holding" role in central midfield: a defensively focused position, where he wins the ball and distributes it effectively with incisive passing. His ability to do this is so good that he is now considered the best male player on the planet, even if he's not blasting in all the goals or dribbling past multiple players very often.

Not every young player can be the star striker; looking at how Rodri plays can unlock another perspective on how to be the most valuable player by knitting together passes and intercepting play in midfield in an astute, thoughtful way.

Sophia Smith

Sometimes child prodigies don't pan out, but sometimes they turn out to be one of the best players in the world. That's the case with Sophia Smith, the Coloradan who was called up to the

U.S. Women's National Team at the tender age of 16 and has been tearing it up for club and country in recent years.

Smith has won the NWSL Championship (named the MVP of the season) and helped lead the United States to the gold medal at the 2024 Olympic Games in Paris. A prolific scoring forward, Smith has pace to burn, superb technical ability, and times her runs with the precision of a fighter jet. She's the type of player who raises the heart rate of anyone watching, ready to do something electric at any moment.

Sometimes players in youth soccer are afraid to take risks and dribble the ball, and all too often, that fear stops players from developing the skills they need to do something unexpected and special with the ball. Have your kid watch Sophia Smith's fearless approach to running with the ball, and it just may inspire them to try something different!

Chapter **18**

Ten Ways to Get Better at Home

The beauty of soccer is that it's one of the easiest games in the world to pick up and play, with lots of ways involving a ball — and not involving a ball — that can help your kid improve their skills at home. Improvement can also come from the mental side of understanding the game and how it is played, which can come on the couch watching YouTube videos or reading an old-fashioned book.

Watch and Analyze Soccer Videos

Any time you can get better at something by sitting on the couch doing it, that's surely a win. You can do this by pulling up some soccer YouTube videos. You can choose from a million instructional videos or just watch highlight reels of top players or big matches.

The point is to sit with your child and spend time proactively talking and analyzing what they see in the play. You don't need to know a lot about soccer — in fact, if you don't, this is a chance to have your kid explain to you what they see and are learning about the game.

Watching soccer action with an eye on understanding why something happens — why a player moves a certain way, or whether a player has made the right decision with the ball — can help develop game intelligence and a sense of what is happening that'll become second nature when they are then playing themselves.

Practice with a Tennis Ball

Isn't a tennis ball too small to practice with? Well, that's kind of the point. If your child can get comfortable kicking and controlling a tennis ball, then when they get on the field with a larger soccer ball, it'll feel as easy as controlling a beach ball.

Many of the best players in the world, like Lionel Messi, grew up kicking around tiny balls. This develops technical skills with the ball.

Anywhere there isn't something you can break with a tennis ball — perhaps a yard or a garage space — kick a tennis ball back and forth with your child. Encourage them to try juggling the ball, which will be hard at first but can quickly get easier. This can even be done in socks or bare feet.

Balancing Acts

Can standing on one leg make your kid better at soccer? Probably, yes! Soccer is a game that is highly dependent on the ability to balance. I'm sure that if Lionel Messi or Ronaldo had been trained as dancers, they'd be among the best in the world.

It can also make for a fun — and funny — challenge to see whether you or your child (and other siblings or family members around) can stand on one leg the longest.

You can even extend this to other fun balancing challenges: maybe the good old egg and spoon race across the dining room!

Wall Ball

Soccer is, at its heart, a simple game. Players who can kick the ball and stop the ball effectively with both feet will quickly become very good at it! A simple way to do this is via repetition, and for that, all you need is a wall your kid can kick the ball against (without breaking anything or annoying the neighbors!).

If you feel comfortable enough, you can also join in for a game of semicompetitive wall ball or encourage your kid to play against their friends. The rules are simple enough: Players take turns kicking the ball against the wall. Whoever misses first loses, and the other player gets a point. First to ten points wins.

The nice part about playing wall ball with another player is that the ball will start coming back at unexpected and different angles, encouraging good movement and anticipation to get the ball back. And it's even more fun!

Read Up on the Game

There are plenty of good reasons for your child to be reading, regardless of whether it makes them better at soccer or not, so there's a double benefit to encouraging your child's love of the game with a supply of books about the sport!

Reading specifically about soccer, though, will undoubtedly deepen their appreciation and love of the game, which may in turn lead them to have a better understanding and greater appreciation of the sport.

Books to read may cover some of the best teams or players in history, and you should be able to find a selection at your local library or, of course, purchase them new or used online. Stories of the greats can be inspirational.

For older kids, you can also find books that delve deep into tactics and strategies. Gaining an understanding of formations and approaches coaches use can enhance how players see the game from a different perspective than simply playing it.

Healthy Habits

I cover some aspects of how to stay healthy in Chapter 7, but it's also really important to think about how to set in motion a chain of good habits that can benefit your kid not just now but for years to come.

You can see Chapter 7 for all the details of what to load up on and when, but the big tip here is to try and get your kid to understand the value of eating well. That doesn't mean a diet of no treats and nothing but lentils and granola.

Instead, just encourage them to see the value of a balanced diet and how it helps provide them energy for the soccer field. Having them feel like a good diet is positive and something they are part of shaping gives those habits a much better chance of sticking for the long run — which will be beneficial on and off the soccer field!

Talk About the Game

There are positive and negative ways to approach discussing how your child is experiencing their play on the field. The negative way is to get into emotional discussions — often right after a match — that focus on what went wrong.

WARNING

Particularly in the first 24 hours after playing, there's little to be gained from forcing a discussion on what went right or wrong in a match. For most kids, it takes time to digest and get things into perspective.

However, if your child does need to let off steam, it's good to listen. And away from the heat right after a match or a tournament, it can be really helpful to think about how the team played, to see if they have thoughts on team tactics or their approach to the game. This type of talk at home can encourage an analytical mindset, enhancing game intelligence and a thoughtful way of playing.

Spend Time Together

Training with the team is structured and planned, following (assuming the coach and club are good!) a carefully constructed curriculum to get better at fundamental techniques and tactics of soccer.

That structured time is great, but so can be unstructured, spontaneous kickarounds with the ball. Especially at the younger ages, you can do this with your child regardless of your own level of soccer skill. Simply head outside in the yard or to a local park and have a kickaround.

Maybe the unstructured play will improve some fundamental techniques, or maybe it will simply be good fun with the ball and a parent or caregiver. Either way, if getting outside and kicking it around provides fun around soccer, it's good for their long-term love of the game.

Juggle to Success

Sometimes the summer holidays can feel long, and you need something to incentivize your kid to get outside and off their device. Why not set a challenge that gets them active and can fundamentally improve their soccer skills?

Juggling the ball — that is, one player kicking the ball and keeping it in the air with repeated kicks without it touching the ground — is proven to be one of the fastest ways for a player to develop their fundamental good touch of the ball.

The key to success is repeated practice. Reward your child for doing ten minutes a day or reaching a certain goal in improving the number of touches they can do. See Chapter 9 for tips on getting your kid juggling the ball successfully.

Control the Ball

Another simple way to get better at home follows the advice of one of the most technically skilled players of all time, the Bulgarian legend and former Manchester United striker Dimitar Berbatov. Berbatov was famed for how deftly he could control a soccer ball flying at home from seemingly any angle or speed, using one touch of a foot like a magic wand to bring it under his spell.

Perhaps Berbatov was naturally gifted with this touch. Or maybe, as he's explained, it was a product of tons of repetition with the ball on his own. Berbatov would throw the ball high in the air repeatedly and work to softly control it, doing so hundreds of times until he was satisfied with his touch. He'd then try different heights and angles, bouncing it off a wall.

If your kid starts working on this, encourage them to use different parts of both feet to control the ball. This can be done at home or a local park with just a ball — a reminder that soccer doesn't have to cost a fortune in time or money to follow some of the training routines of the game's greats!

Chapter **19**

Ten Ways to Follow Planet Soccer

As your kid gets into soccer, they'll likely start to explore the global world of soccer as a fan. Some of the top players in the world are icons with more followers than any other human on social media, and some of the teams have fan bases hundreds of millions strong worldwide. Getting familiar with these players, teams, and the competitions they take part in can help you and your kid dive deeper into the sport, strengthening interest and passion — and just as importantly, opening up a new world of exciting fandom. Here are ten ways to fast forward into following along with Planet Soccer!

Watch a World Cup

The FIFA World Cup, for male national teams, and the FIFA Women's World Cup, for female national teams, are considered the pinnacles of global soccer. Note that the men's and women's editions are entirely separate competitions, staged in different years on four-year cycles.

Starting with the 2026 tournament, which takes place in North America (including in 11 American cities), 48 nations will compete in the men's World Cup finals tournament. In 2027, 32 teams will take part in the women's World Cup equivalent, set to be hosted by Brazil.

World Cup tournaments are a great time and opportunity to really get into soccer. The energy and excitement around the nations of the world competing to reach the pinnacle of the sport in a short, sharp competition showcases some of the best action in the sport.

Go to a Game

Going to a soccer game live with your child can bring the game to life in a new way: seeing the swell of support for the home team, or appreciating the skill and physicality of professional players in the flesh.

The premier professional leagues to follow in America are the National Women's Soccer League (NWSL) on the women's side and Major League Soccer (MLS), the men's counterpart. Each are nationwide leagues, though not every city boasts both an MLS and NWSL team (though some are lucky enough to have both).

Fear not if your area doesn't feature an MLS or NWSL team: There's an increasing proliferation of professional teams to follow in cities large and small around the country. Check out leagues under the United Soccer Leagues (USL) umbrella or even high-level college soccer. You might just see a star in the making! If your child is playing youth soccer, there'll often be a group outing you can join with your kid and teammates heading out to a professional match together, which is a great communal experience.

Pick a Premier League Club

The most popular professional league in the world is probably England's Premier League, which features famous teams you may hear about — Manchester United, Manchester City, Liverpool, Arsenal, and Chelsea are probably the best known. Each has a rich history of winning silverware and boast millions of followers around the world, including in the United States.

The time difference with England (five hours ahead of the east coast) means fans of these teams, or those who just enjoy an all-action Premier League matchup, are tuning in early most weekend mornings to watch their teams. NBC currently holds the broadcast rights to Premier League soccer in the United States, showing pretty much every game across their network, cable, and streaming platforms, so there'll be more action to follow than you can keep up with if you get into it.

So who should you follow? The big clubs I mention previously tend to hoover up a lot of support because they're more likely to win trophies than most other clubs. However, there's plenty of rich history, interesting stories, and great players at lots of other English teams, so perhaps take some time to soak in some action and see who appeals to you!

. . . Or a Team from Elsewhere!

Planet Soccer is enormous, and though a lot of world soccer news (especially in the English language) can revolve around England's Premier League, it's a long way from being as dominant in the sport as, say, the NFL is in American football.

Fans of Spanish soccer will rightly argue its top teams — Real Madrid and Barcelona — have been stronger in European competition and featured more superstars than their English competition on balance over the past couple of decades.

Meanwhile, Germany boasts a winning machine in Bayern Munich as well as a vibrant fan culture that is a sight to behold following teams like Borussia Dortmund. The Italian league has an incredibly rich history, while France is known as producing a pipeline of remarkably talented young players.

And that's just a Eurocentric view. The culture and passion of South American football stands out, and in fact, every continent has a fascinating set of teams, players, and histories to explore.

There's not even a reason to go overseas to follow a team. I mention earlier the fun to be had following your local team in leagues like MLS (which also feature Canadian teams) and the NWSL, and top-tier Mexican teams enjoy a massive following in many parts of America.

Screen Some Live Action

Because soccer is a global sport, you can almost always find a broadcast of a top-level game happening somewhere in the world every day. The biggest competitions and leagues have broadcast deals on prominent network, cable, and streaming platforms, though the more obscure matches take a little more hunting to track down.

The easiest and cheapest way to watch games is when they are broadcast on "free-to-air" channels, such as your local network ABC, NBC, FOX, or CBS affiliate station, which doesn't require any payment or subscription. These stations are not chock-full of soccer action, but there'll often be a couple of games each weekend you can check out.

Broadcast rights deals shift frequently, but at the time of writing, NBC broadcasts the English Premier League on its national network (usually one game a week during the season) and CBS shows the National Women's Soccer League (NWSL).

The bulk of Planet Soccer is shown on an ever-increasing variety of subscription services. You may already be subscribed to one or more of these services for other content, or you may need to start a new subscription. For example, NBC's premium Peacock streaming service includes access to a large number of English Premier League games (over 175 per season) in addition to the movies, TV shows, and other sports available on the platform. The top German league, Bundesliga, is on the ESPN+ service, as is Spain's premier league, La Liga, which features two of the giants of the game, Real Madrid and Barcelona. Europe's top continent-wide competition, the UEFA Champions League, is shown on Paramount+.

Every single Major League Soccer game is shown on Apple TV. However, even if you already are an Apple TV subscriber, you need to purchase an additional "MLS Season Pass" to view the games.

The National Women's Soccer League is shown on multiple platforms, meaning that to follow every game, you need to purchase subscriptions to various services, including ESPN and Paramount+, in addition to viewing games shown free on CBS and ION TV.

Catch the Highlights

Let's be real: Sitting down for 90 minutes of a match in addition to also driving the kids to actually go and play soccer can often be a bit much to ask. Fortunately — and not to be too reductive about it — soccer is largely about the handful of goals and near misses each game features, so you can keep up with the big moments and brilliant plays with highlight packages.

There are two main types of highlight packages. The first are game recaps that are usually posted by broadcasters not long after games end. Where you can find these depends on the myriad of broadcasting rights situations for different competitions, which I cover in the earlier section "Screen Some Live Action."

Find who broadcasts your favorite league, and you can usually find game highlights on their platforms. For example, Apple holds the rights to Major League Soccer, and you'll find game highlights as well as the live broadcasts on the Apple TV app or website.

The second type of highlight package is most commonly found on YouTube: fan compilations of some of the best, funniest, or craziest moments in world soccer. Type "soccer highlights" into YouTube and see what rabbit holes you end up going down. There are certainly tons of fun packages that put together great goals and classic moments from matches more recent and from the distant past, which can be a great way to learn about the game now as well as its history.

Follow on Your Phone

Keeping track of everything in Planet Soccer is about as realistic as keeping up with everything happening on Planet Earth, but fortunately there are lots of apps that can help you keep track of the teams, leagues, players, and news from around the world in a personalized and curated way.

To find out what to tune in to and watch, there are many websites and apps that can help you keep track of which games are being broadcasted where. Try www.livesoccertv.com or www.worldsoccertalk.com for schedules.

Live score apps such as FotMob also list where each game is being broadcast. FotMob can keep you up to date by the second on scores from pretty much any game around the world, as do competitors such as SofaScoer and Flashscore. These apps also let you set certain teams or leagues as favorites, so you see scores from those at the top of the feed and can customize receiving goal and score alerts if you want your phone to be buzzing away.

Live score apps also usually cover the latest news in soccer, though you may want to explore some deeper editorial websites for stronger coverage. The Guardian (www.theguardian.com) and The Athletic (www.theathletic.com) both have comprehensive news and feature coverage of European and American leagues (though note that The Athletic is a subscription service owned by the *New York Times*).

Cheer for Team America

Any time a major international competition such as a World Cup comes along, it can be a lot of fun to break out the red, white, and blue clothing and root for America on the global stage. The United States is represented by a number of teams internationally, most prominently by the women's and men's adult national teams.

The U.S. Women's National Team (USWNT) is one of the most successful teams in the history of the sport in either gender. Since the first official FIFA Women's World Cup was held in 1991, the USA team has won four of the nine tournaments contested, along with gold medals in the Olympic Games in the same time frame. No other international team can come close to boasting this level of success.

Tuning in to watch the American women's national team play means watching some of the best players in the world. The United States Men's National Team has not been as successful as its female counterpart. The men's team has never won a World Cup or even reached the finals. The United States simply doesn't have as many world class players on the men's side. The American team is certainly competitive, though, and has frequently reached the last 16 knockout stage of the World Cup. And in 2026, the United States will be one of the co-hosts, so here's hoping for a fairy-tale run you can follow through the competition.

Video Game Soccer

What's driven the growth in popularity of soccer in America over the past couple of decades? There are lots of reasons for this, but one is the millions who have learned about the game from playing it on video games. The most popular for many years has been what is now called "EA Sports FC" but was for a long time called "FIFA" (until a licensing agreement with the sport's global governing body expired).

EA Sports FC is best known as a console game on the Xbox and PlayStation platforms, though it's now available in a mobile-friendly format for your phone as well.

If you're a gamer, it's definitely worth checking out EA Sports FC, where you take control of a team (with thousands of real teams, players, and stadiums in the game) and can play against the computer, match up online with someone from around the world, or see whether you can beat your kid playing head-to-head on the couch!

Settle Down for a Soccer Show

Speaking of the couch, that's a great place to relax and dig into soccer movies and documentaries. As you'd expect, you can find shows and films about all aspects of global soccer culture and history.

Want to go behind the scenes with some of the top soccer clubs in the world? There are plenty of documentaries that follow the players and coaches throughout the season, such as Amazon's *All or Nothing* series that covers the likes of Tottenham Hotspur, Manchester City, and Borussia Dortmund.

But perhaps the most famous and interesting entry into this genre is *Welcome to Wrexham*, which has followed the Welsh club since it was purchased by movie star Ryan Reynolds and TV star Rob McElhenney. This has led to quite a Hollywood story of their rise.

For some comedy, there's the breakthrough hit *Ted Lasso* (played by Jason Segel), the story of an American football manager tasked with coaching a Premier League soccer team in London. There's lots of soccer action, but the best part is the humor and sentimentality that shine through in just the right way.

Glossary

Advantage: An *advantage* is given by a referee allowing play to continue even after a foul has been committed because stopping the game would actually disadvantage the team on the receiving end of a foul (infringement). This gives the team with the ball the opportunity to maintain possession and attack rather than stopping the play immediately for a free kick, which might negatively impact them. The referee signals an advantage by waving in a forward motion to the players on the field.

Assist: The *assist* goes to the player who plays a pass that directly leads to a goal being scored by another player. This recognizes the skill in setting up a goal.

Assistant coach: Supports the coach in training the team and managing them on game day. Assistant coaches help in various ways to prepare the team, running drills and working on strategy. Youth teams won't always have assistant coaches, but professional teams always do.

Assistant referee: You'll see them running down the sideline, which is why in the past, assistant referees were known as *linesmen* or *lineswomen*. This official supports the referee, assisting with various aspects of the game. Assistant referees help with decisions such as calling offsides and fouls as well as determining possession for throw-ins, corner kicks, and goal kicks.

Bench: Being on the bench on the sideline means the player is not currently on the field of play. Usually, players on the bench are waiting for their chance to get onto the field by substituting (replacing) another player currently on the field.

Booking: It's not good to get in the referee's book! This means that the referee has disciplined a player and made a note of it in their *book* for committing an infringement. A first booking results in a *yellow card* being shown (essentially a caution) and a second booking in the same game results in a *red card* for the player, which means expulsion from the field for the rest of the game.

Captain: A team's leader on the field. In professional soccer, the captain is expected to lead by example and inspire the rest of the team, as well as being the primary point of contact with the referee. In youth soccer, this role is often rotated among players across multiple games to give various players the chance to assume the role.

Center spot: At the precise center of a soccer field sits the center spot, where you'll see the game begin every time — with the ball kicked from that exact point marked by a small painted circle. It's also where play restarts from after a goal and for the start of the second half.

Clean sheet: Nobody likes dirty sheets! That's the origin of the phrase *clean sheet* to denote when a team does not blemish its record in a game by conceding any goals. Credit is usually directed in this case to the goalkeeper and defensive unit.

Cleats: No youth soccer player can get very far without *cleats,* specialized shoes that provide traction, stability, and comfort to stay grounded on grass or an artificial surface. Cleats are made with studs on the sole to help players grip the ground and are shaped to help with good connections when striking or controlling the ball.

Coach: The person most responsible for a youth soccer team's development: leading training sessions to develop players' skills, selecting the team and tactics, and working to motivate and inspire players.

Corner kick: As its name explains literally, this is a kick taken from one of the four corners of the soccer field. It takes place to restart play for the attacking team after the ball goes over the goal line, if last touched by a player from the defending team. Occasionally a goal is scored when directly kicked into the goal from a corner kick; this memorable moment is known as an *Olimpico.*

Crossbar: Straddling the top of the goal itself is a horizontal bar known as the *crossbar,* which is connected to the two vertical posts that make up the main part of the goal frame. Its height varies in youth soccer (lower for younger ages), up to a full-size height of 8 feet.

Defender: Preventing goals is the primary objective for players positioned as defenders. They play in front of the goalkeeper, intercepting the ball and stopping attacks by tackling the opposition.

Draw: This game result has sometimes been seen as controversial in American sports culture. A *draw* is another name for a tie, something that doesn't happen often in most American sports. In soccer, during regular season league play, draws are fairly common when each team scores the same number of goals in a game. Each team is usually awarded one point.

Dribble: Watching a soccer player weave past opponents with the ball seemingly glued to their feet is one of the joys of the game and defines the art known as *dribbling*. Deft touches are used to control and maneuver the ball past and around other players, an important part of attacking play.

Extra time: If the scores are tied at the end of regulation time, a period of *extra time* can be added to try to determine a winning team. During regular season play, extra time isn't usually added; it's typically deployed when there is elimination play in tournaments to ensure that a winner is found. If the score is still tied after extra time, a penalty shootout follows.

First touch: When the ball comes to a player, the first touch they take making contact with the ball is critical to effectively make the next move — whether passing, shooting, or dribbling the ball. A good first touch brings the ball under close control close to the player, giving them more time to make the next move. A bad first touch may see the ball bounce away from the player, potentially to the opposition.

Formation: The way players line up on the field during play is referred to as a *formation*. A series of numbers is used to refer to how the players are arranged into attacking and defending positions. For example, a "4-4-2" means there are four defenders, four midfielders, and two attackers. Note that this only adds up to 10 players, not 11: That's because the goalkeeping position is fixed in place, so it isn't listed in formations numerically.

Foul: Breaking a rule in soccer, particularly when impeding an opposing player, is referred to as a *foul*. Illegal actions, such as kicking, tripping, holding or pushing an opponent, and handling the ball, are penalized with a free kick or penalty being awarded to the other team. A serious foul may result in a yellow or red card being shown to the infringing player.

Free kick: Following a foul play by a team, a *free kick* is awarded to the opposing team. This means they will take an unopposed kick from a set spot on the field where the foul was committed, with the infringing team having to line up at least 10 yards from the ball. Free kicks can either be direct or indirect, depending on the type of offense committed. *Direct kicks* can be kicked straight at the goal, while *indirect kicks* must be touched by a second player before going in the goal.

Friendly: Often called an exhibition or scrimmage in American sports parlance, *friendlies* are games taking place outside of formal competitions. They are usually played to provide further practice for the teams with nothing formal riding on the result.

Goal: The purpose of soccer is to score more goals (points) than the opposition in a given game. This is done by getting the ball into the opposition's goal, all the way across the line that is marked between the two posts and underneath the crossbar.

Goal kick: After the ball crosses the line running along either side of the goal, it is restarted by the defending team with a goal kick if it had last been touched by an attacking player. The ball is kicked into play by the defending team, usually by the goalkeeper, from inside the 6-yard box in front of the goal.

Half: "Soccer is a game of two halves" is an old clichéd phrase in Britain but is almost always literally true: Each game is divided into two equal-length periods of play with a break in between. Halves in professional soccer last 45 minutes, though in youth soccer they are shorter and depend on the age of the children (shorter halves for younger children).

Halftime: Break out the orange slices! The interval between the first half and second half is called *halftime* and it's a chance for the players to take a breather, receive some coaching advice, get some hydration, and — in traditional youth soccer culture — chow down on some orange slices brought by the parents.

Handball: Soccer is played with the feet (or sometimes with the head, chest, or other body parts) but never with the hands — except for the goalkeeper, of course. Deliberately handling the ball, or even accidentally doing so in ways that secure an unfair advantage in play, is against the rules.

Hat trick: Soccer is a low-scoring game. Any individual player scoring a goal or two in one game is an achievement in itself. If one player scores three goals in one game, that is considered an extra-special achievement and is designated as a *hat trick*.

Header: Contacting the ball with the head is given the straightforward name of a *header*. A technically correct header is performed using the forehead and can be used to score goals, pass the ball, or clear the ball away defensively. Because of the contact with the head, kids aren't typically allowed to head the ball until age 11 or older (different states have different rules on this).

Keeper: A shortened version of "goalkeeper." Sometimes called the "goalie" for short as well.

Kickoff: Play in soccer — to start a match, after a goal, or after halftime — begins with a kickoff from the center spot in the middle of the field.

Match: Another name for a game, especially used in British soccer.

Midfielder: Roaming the middle of the field, midfield players are important in both defensive and offensive aspects of the game. Typically, they need to be able to both pass well to link up attacks and tackle well to defend against the opposition.

Nutmeg: This is a special name given to the relatively infrequent moments when a player intentionally plays the ball through the legs of an opponent and keeps possession of it by then regaining the ball on the other side. It's a fun move that needs to be timed well and is made even better in pickup play if accompanied by a shout of "nutmeg" when making the move.

Offside: One of the more difficult terms to summarize but one you will hear a lot, an *offside* is essentially called if a player is in a position considered illegal in the rules when the ball is passed toward them. Illegal positions include being closer to the opponent's goal than both the ball and two defending players (including the goalkeeper) or gaining an advantage by being in an offside position.

Own goal: Usually being credited with scoring a goal is a good thing, but that's not the case when a player accidentally sends the ball into their own's team net — an *own goal*. This can happen from a misdirected kick or a deflection that sends the ball into the goal unintentionally.

Pass: One of the building blocks of the game, the act of passing the ball to a teammate — usually by kicking it to them — helps a team retain possession and control the play. A pass that leads directly to a goal being scored is called an assist.

Penalty area: The rectangle surrounding each goal, the *penalty area* is where the hottest action in soccer takes place as teams try to score and stop goals. It's also the area where if a foul is committed by the defending team, a penalty kick is awarded to the attacking team.

Penalty kick: A foul committed by the defending team in their own penalty area results in a *penalty kick* for the attacking team. This unopposed kick is taken from the penalty spot, with the attacker attempting to strike the ball (with one kick) past the goalkeeper. No defenders are allowed to be in the penalty area. Penalty kicks usually, but not always, result in a goal being scored.

Penalty shootout: If the score is tied at the end of an elimination game, a *penalty shootout* is often used to determine a winning team. Each team will alternate taking five penalty kicks, with the team that scores the most from those five advancing. Players taking the kicks must have been on the field playing when the final whistle ending the game blew.

Pitch: The playing field, often called a *pitch* in soccer.

Red card: The most serious disciplinary action in a game results in a player receiving a *red card* and being sent off (ejected) for the rest of the match. Their team must therefore play with one less player for the remainder of the game.

Referee: The person in charge of enforcing the rules on the field to ensure fair play. The referee has the final say on all decisions related to maintaining order, safety, and ensuring the rules are followed during the game.

Save: When a goalkeeper stops the ball from going into the goal, it is called a *save* (as in "saving a goal from being scored").

Scrimmage: Scrimmages, or informal games, can be organized within practice sessions by teams or as separate practice matches between teams. They are typically used to help prepare players for organized matches.

Set piece: When play is restarted after a stoppage (such as a foul), the resulting opportunity for the attacking team to attempt an organized attacking play is known as a *set piece.* The best set piece opportunities usually come from free kicks in the opponent's half or from corner kicks.

Shot: Typically the way a goal is scored, a *shot* is an attempt on goal by an attacking player, usually from a kick or header.

Stoppage time: With some exceptions, the referee does not end the game exactly when the allotted time for the match has ended; additional *stoppage time* is added at their discretion to take into account delays during the game that interrupted play. This may be due to time being lost for treatment of injuries, substitutions, or any time-wasting by players.

Striker: Often the player who gets the most glory is the one who scores the goal, and most often that's someone playing the role of *striker* — charged with putting the ball into the back of the net. The striker typically positions themself close to the opponent's goal, ready to finish chances that come their way to get their team on the score sheet.

Substitute: Sitting on the sideline at the start of the game, *substitutes* are players not selected in the starting lineup who are available to enter the game later and replace another player. The coach may substitute a player in because of injuries, tactics, energy levels, or most commonly in the case of youth soccer, to ensure that players are rotated and get a chance to play. In youth soccer, unlimited substitutions are allowed in most competitive matches, and players can exit and reenter during the same game multiple times. At higher levels of play, there will be limitations in the number of substitutions allowed.

Tackle: A tackle in soccer isn't quite the same as in American football: You can't grapple an opponent to the floor. Instead, tackling is usually done with the feet to challenge the opponent who has the ball and strip it from them.

Throw-in: When the ball goes out of bounds over either of the sidelines that make up the longer lines of a rectangular soccer field, play is restarted with a *throw-in*. It's taken by the team that did not last touch the ball before it went over the sideline.

Tie: Also known as a draw, when a game ends without a winning team being declared because the score in number of goals by each team is tied.

Volley: Often resulting in spectacular plays when pulled off, a *volley* is the name given when the ball is kicked in the air by a player before it touches the ground. This takes great timing and good technique to execute well!

Wall: When an attacking team is lining up to take a free kick at a distance close enough for a direct shot on goal, the defensive team will often line up a *wall* of players standing next to each other. They are placed there to try to block the ball from reaching the goal and make it difficult to score.

Wing: The *wing* is the part of the field flanking the left and right sides, giving the name *winger* to attacking players who operate in this area.

Yellow card: A player may receive a disciplinary "caution" for an offense that means they are shown a *yellow card*. If they are shown a second yellow card, they also automatically receive a red card and are ejected from the game. Yellow cards are given for behavior deemed a serious infraction of the rules, such as a dangerous foul, dissent to the referee, or a deliberate handball.

Index

C

California, junior colleges in, 214
California Community College Athletic Association (CCCAA), 214
calls, for referees, 69
calm, staying, 135
Camp Nou (Barcelona), 237
camps, 38–40
captain, 266
carbohydrates, for pre-game nutrition, 119
cardio, 123
carpooling, for competitive club soccer, 100–101
CCCAA (California Community College Athletic Association), 214
center back, 16
center forward, 16
center spot, 266
challenges, managing, 221–229
Cheat Sheet (website), 3
cheering, 104–105
clean sheet, 266
cleats, 44–46, 266
clock, 17
club camps, 179
club soccer. See competitive club soccer
club soccer (college), 214–215
coaches
    communications with, 92, 93, 224–225
    contacting via email, 218–219
    defined, 266
    evaluation of, 107
    experiences of, for competitive club soccer programs, 82
    for goalkeepers, 145
    positions and, 223–224
coaching. See also parent coaching
    approaches to, 222–225
    for competitive club soccer, 76
    as a consideration for signing up for next season, 108–109
    style and strategy, 222–223
cold weather gear, 47
college club soccer, 214–215
college showcases, 218
college soccer
    about, 198–199, 209

getting recruited for, 215–219
    levels for, 209–215
    scholarships, 219
college-based camps, 179–180
committing to academy soccer, 199–201
communication
    assessing at tryouts, 86
    with coaches, 93
    with parents, 54–55
    with the team, 140–141
competition, in academy soccer, 199–200
competitive club soccer
    about, 73–74, 91–92
    assessing current season, 106–107
    carpooling, 100–101
    coach communication, 92, 93
    committing to, 74–76
    expectations for, 76–78
    facilities for, 95
    game and practice schedules for, 98–99
    juggling high school soccer and, 190–191
    juggling school soccer and, 189–190
    key contacts for, 93–95
    paying to play, 87–90
    recreational programs compared with, 74, 79
    safety in, 112–115
    selecting programs, 78–87
    sideline behavior, 103–106
    signing up for next season, 108–112
    tournaments for, 99–100
    uniforms for, 97–98
    volunteering for, 96–97
    weather and, 101–103
compression, for bruises, 126
concentration, for goalkeeping, 141–142
concussion protocols, 130–131
cone drills, 155–156
cones, for parent coaches, 54
contacts
    coaches via email, 218–219
    in competitive club soccer, 93–95
contests, international, 234
controlling the ball, 256
controlling the midfield, camps for, 185
contusions, 125–127
cool down, 130

F

facilities, for competitive club teams, 80, 95
feedback, 106–107
fees
  for camps, 40
  for competitive club soccer programs, 83
  as a program consideration, 32
  for specialized training camps, 183–184
  for trainers, 164
females
  top competitions for girls, 202–203
  top overseas leagues for, 232–233
field conditions, weather and, 102–103
field of play, 12–13
FIFA World Cup, 234, 257–258, 263
first touch, 267
fit, for shoes, 43
fitness, as a benefit of youth soccer, 9–11.
  See also health
fitness, speed, and agility camps, 186
fitness programs
  about, 121
  for teenagers, 122–124
  for under-12s, 121–122
5-a-side soccer, 175
fixo, for futsal, 172–173
Flashscore app, 262
focusing on finishing, camps for, 185
footwork, for goalkeeping, 145
formation, 267
FotMob app, 262
fouls, 21–23, 267
fractures, 128–129
free kick, 267
freestyle fun and games, 161–162
friendly, 267
friendship, as a benefit of youth soccer, 8–9
fruits, for pre-game nutrition, 119
full back, 16
fun, as a benefit of youth soccer, 8–9
fundamentals, for elite academy recruits, 206
futsal
  about, 45, 169
  ball for, 171
  court for, 170
  finding programs, 173
  history of, 169–170
  positions and skills, 172–173
  rules for, 171–172

G

GA (Girls Academy), 202–203
gametime
  assessing game understanding at tryouts, 86
  game management, 64–66
  game schedules for competitive club soccer, 98–99
  gear, 46–48
  for recreational teams, 36
  referee checks of length of, 67–68
  shoes, 43–46
  sidelines, 48–50
  uniform, 41–42
Garnier, Séan (professional player), 161–162
gear. See equipment
Girls Academy (GA), 202–203
gloves, for goalkeeping, 143–144
goal (soccer), 267–268
goal kick, 24–25, 268
goal lines, 12
goalkeepers, 14, 16, 42
goalkeeping
  about, 137
  basics of, 138–142
  camps for, 186
  concentration for, 141–142
  distributing the ball, 139–140
  equipment for, 142–144
  for futsal, 172
  loneliness of, 146–147
  making saves, 139
  specialized training programs, 144–146
  team communication, 140–141
goals, for parent coaches, 54
grass, footwear for, 44
Grassroots Coaching, 52
group communication, for parent coaching, 55
The Guardian, 262

H

half, 268
halftime, 268
handball, 268
hat trick, 268
Hayes, Bob (professional athlete), 164
header, 268
headgear, 47–48
health. *See also* fitness
  about, 117
  fitness programs, 121–124
  managing nutrition, 118–121
  mental, 133–136
healthy habits, 254
height, 10, 138
high school soccer, 190–194
highlight packages, 261–262
highlight reel, 215–217
history
  of competitive club soccer programs, 82–83
  of futsal, 169–170
holding midfielder, 16
home uniform, 42
Horan, Lindsey (professional player), 245–246
hydration
  for post-game nutrition, 120
  for pre-game nutrition, 119

I

ice, for bruises, 126
icons, explained, 3
ID camps, 180
indirect free kick, 23
indoor/gym, footwear for, 45
injuries
  about, 117, 124–125
  concussion protocols, 130–131
  contusions, 125–127
  managing, 124–130
  minor, 125–127
  preventing, 129–130
  recovering from concussions, 132–133
  serious, 128–129
  substitutions due to, 25
international club-run camps, 180–181

J

Jackson, Bo (professional athlete), 164
jerseys, 42, 142–143
juggling, 153–155, 255–256
junior college, 213–214
junior varsity (JV), 192–193

K

keeper, 268
kickoff, 268
kid to coach ratio, as a program consideration, 31
knee injuries, 128, 129

L

La Liga (Spain), 233, 261
leagues, elite, 201–205
length of play, 17
level of play
  for college soccer, 209–215
  for competitive club soccer programs, 78, 81
light activity, as a recovery stage, 132
Ligue 1 (France), 233
Lil' Kickers, 31
linesmen, 265
lineswomen, 265
live games, international, 237–238, 258
live score apps, 262
local youth club camps, 179
location, as a program consideration, 32
loneliness, of goalkeeping, 146–147

M

Major League Soccer (MLS), 201, 258, 261
males
  top competitions for boys, 203–204
  top overseas leagues for, 233–234

About the Author

Tom Dunmore is the author of multiple publications including *Soccer For Dummies* and a *Historical Dictionary of Soccer* and has been a contributor to numerous publications including ESPN Grantland and USSoccer.com.

Tom has worked extensively in American soccer and other sports as an executive with over 15 years of experience leading marketing and communications teams.

Based in Denver, Tom loves to enjoy the outdoors with his family, chasing his sons Jack and Jonny down the ski slopes and hiking trails of Colorado — when they're not playing soccer!

Dedication

The author would like to dedicate this book to his children and youth soccer players, Jack and Jonny, who continue to provide a great real-world education in the sport. It's a pleasure for Tom and his wife Monika to watch their love of the sport grow as they navigate the game together!

Author's Acknowledgments

The author would like to thank the incredible For Dummies team for the guidance throughout this project, especially Jennifer Yee, who has been a rock on three different *For Dummies* books. And Chrissy Guthrie, for her patience and insight developing the content, along with Paul Levesque in the early days of the work. Thanks as well to Christy Pingleton for assistance with copyediting and Dave Beck for his work as the technical editor.

Publisher's Acknowledgments

Senior Acquisitions Editor:
Jennifer Yee

Development Editor:
Christina Guthrie

Copy Editor: Christine Pingleton

Production Editor:
Tamilmani Varadharaj

Managing Editor: Ajith Kumar

Cover Image: © kali9/Getty Images

Leverage the power

Dummies is the global leader in the reference category and one of the most trusted and highly regarded brands in the world. No longer just focused on books, customers now have access to the dummies content they need in the format they want. Together we'll craft a solution that engages your customers, stands out from the competition, and helps you meet your goals.

Advertising & Sponsorships

Connect with an engaged audience on a powerful multimedia site, and position your message alongside expert how-to content. Dummies.com is a one-stop shop for free, online information and know-how curated by a team of experts.

- Targeted ads
- Video
- Email Marketing
- Microsites
- Sweepstakes sponsorship

20 **MILLION** PAGE VIEWS EVERY SINGLE MONTH

15 MILLION **UNIQUE** VISITORS PER MONTH

43% OF ALL VISITORS ACCESS THE SITE VIA THEIR MOBILE DEVICES

700,000 NEWSLETTER SUBSCRIPTIONS TO THE INBOXES OF

300,000 UNIQUE INDIVIDUALS EVERY WEEK

# of dummies

Custom Publishing

Reach a global audience in any language by creating a solution that will differentiate you from competitors, amplify your message, and encourage customers to make a buying decision.

- Apps
- Books
- eBooks
- Video
- Audio
- Webinars

Brand Licensing & Content

Leverage the strength of the world's most popular reference brand to reach new audiences and channels of distribution.

For more information, visit **dummies.com/biz**

PERSONAL ENRICHMENT

Staying Sharp
9781119187790
USA $26.00
CAN $31.99
UK £19.99

Facebook
9781119179030
USA $21.99
CAN $25.99
UK £16.99

Guitar
9781119293354
USA $24.99
CAN $29.99
UK £17.99

Investing
9781119293347
USA $22.99
CAN $27.99
UK £16.99

Beekeeping
9781119310068
USA $22.99
CAN $27.99
UK £16.99

Digital Photography
9781119235606
USA $24.99
CAN $29.99
UK £17.99

Meditation
9781119251163
USA $24.99
CAN $29.99
UK £17.99

Pregnancy
9781119235491
USA $26.99
CAN $31.99
UK £19.99

Samsung Galaxy S7
9781119279952
USA $24.99
CAN $29.99
UK £17.99

iPhone
9781119283133
USA $24.99
CAN $29.99
UK £17.99

Crocheting
9781119287117
USA $24.99
CAN $29.99
UK £16.99

Nutrition
9781119130246
USA $22.99
CAN $27.99
UK £16.99

PROFESSIONAL DEVELOPMENT

Windows 10
9781119311041
USA $24.99
CAN $29.99
UK £17.99

AutoCAD
9781119255796
USA $39.99
CAN $47.99
UK £27.99

Excel 2016
9781119293439
USA $26.99
CAN $31.99
UK £19.99

QuickBooks 2017
9781119281467
USA $26.99
CAN $31.99
UK £19.99

macOS Sierra
9781119280651
USA $29.99
CAN $35.99
UK £21.99

LinkedIn
9781119251132
USA $24.99
CAN $29.99
UK £17.99

Windows 1
978111931056
USA $34.00
CAN $41.99
UK £24.99

SharePoint 2016
9781119181705
USA $29.99
CAN $35.99
UK £21.99

Fundamental Analysis
9781119263593
USA $26.99
CAN $31.99
UK £19.99

Networking
9781119257769
USA $29.99
CAN $35.99
UK £21.99

Office 2016
9781119293477
USA $26.99
CAN $31.99
UK £19.99

Office 365
9781119265313
USA $24.99
CAN $29.99
UK £17.99

Salesforce.com
9781119239314
USA $29.99
CAN $35.99
UK £21.99

Coding
9781119929332
USA $29.99
CAN $35.99
UK £21.99

dummies.com

dummies
A Wiley Brand

Learning Made Easy

ACADEMIC

9781119293576
USA $19.99
CAN $23.99
UK £15.99

9781119293637
USA $19.99
CAN $23.99
UK £15.99

9781119293491
USA $19.99
CAN $23.99
UK £15.99

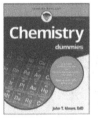

9781119293460
USA $19.99
CAN $23.99
UK £15.99

9781119293590
USA $19.99
CAN $23.99
UK £15.99

9781119215844
USA $26.99
CAN $31.99
UK £19.99

9781119293378
USA $22.99
CAN $27.99
UK £16.99

9781119293521
USA $19.99
CAN $23.99
UK £15.99

9781119239178
USA $18.99
CAN $22.99
UK £14.99

9781119263883
USA $26.99
CAN $31.99
UK £19.99

Available Everywhere Books Are Sold

Small books for big imaginations

9781119177173
USA $9.99
CAN $9.99
UK £8.99

9781119177272
USA $9.99
CAN $9.99
UK £8.99

9781119177241
USA $9.99
CAN $9.99
UK £8.99

9781119177210
USA $9.99
CAN $9.99
UK £8.99

9781119262657
USA $9.99
CAN $9.99
UK £6.99

9781119291336
USA $9.99
CAN $9.99
UK £6.99

9781119233527
USA $9.99
CAN $9.99
UK £6.99

9781119291220
USA $9.99
CAN $9.99
UK £6.99

9781119177302
USA $9.99
CAN $9.99
UK £8.99

Unleash Their Creativity